Seasonal
Salads

Seasonal
Salads

KITCHEN
PRESS

First published in the UK in 2023 by

Kitchen Press Ltd
1 Windsor Place
Dundee
DD2 1BG

Text © Fi Buchanan

Photography by Alan Donaldson

Illustrations © David McDiarmid

Cover design by Sam Paton

Designed by Andrew Forteath

A CIP catalogue record for this book is available from the British Library.

ISBN: 9781916316584

2 3 4 5 6 7 8 9 10

Printed in India

I remember where I was the first time I had rocket: age 10, in corduroys and wellies, at Edna Whyte and Audrey Stone's incredible gallery and restaurant, the Buttery, on the Hebridean island of Luing. I ate for the first time salad that was entirely something other than the token quarter tomato, piece of cucumber and shred of iceberg lettuce. I was struck by lightning. Peppery rocket with homemade brown bread and butter and freshly made lemonade. It was the best meal of my life.

Forty years on, I still find salads just as lip-smacking. They can be anything you want them to be – charred, roasted, sprinkled with sherbet or anointed with herby oils – but should always be fresh, nutritious and reflect the changing seasons.

In the pages that follow you'll find salad classics, new twists on old favourites and exciting foundations to build on so you can create irresistibly delicious meals you will want to eat every day of the year.

In the process of writing this book it has struck me that I experience combinations of flavours as splashes of colour, sparkles, audible pops and bass tracks. To me, salads are composed of elements like a song is composed of chords. I don't think I'm alone; in fact, anyone can experience a salad like this, looking for harmony, then enjoying the taste of it. Take a veg/fruity base, add flavour with fresh greens, herbs and dressing, and enhance the texture with a sprinkle of something crunchy, or a dollop of something refreshingly cool.

Introd

My recipes are just starting points; there are no hard and fast rules when making a salad. Feel free to stray from the ingredients list and cook creatively to please yourself. Treat these recipes as trustworthy bases – enjoy them as they are or be inspired to create your own variations around them. See Delicious Additions on page 136 and Choosing Leaves on page 140 for more free-styling ideas.

Before you start, these truths should be considered:

Developing a repertoire of delicious everyday salads that generate little washing up and happen quickly is cost effective, and healthier than relying on micro-ready meals. And salads are not just for summer; they're a great way to eat all year round.

A good basic pantry is the backbone of a kitchen. Keep on standby a small palette of spices and trusted staples, lemons and limes, a few pots of herbs on the windowsill and a good-value fruity olive oil and this will make the whole cooking process simple and more enjoyable.

Every time when you're cooking – no exceptions – flavour beats finesse. That's to say, when you concentrate on flavour, the finished plate is bound to look delicious.

Remember, music is to cooking as art is to a beautiful interior. I have made seasonal kitchen playlists for enhanced happiness. You should too.

Have fun.

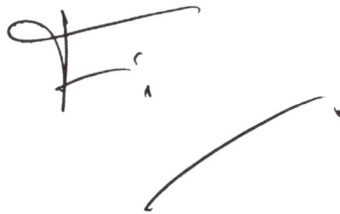

uction

This is the month of new beginnings, one eye on the past and the other on the future. The end of party season and the start of quiet nights in. This is the month for eating comfortingly spiced vegetables and savouring fresh dark greens and tender roots.

January

Roast Sweet Potatoes with Chermoula

You could easily use roasting potatoes in place of the sweet variety here. This is a favourite in our household as, since the oven's on anyway, it's easy to add in a protein of your choice to turn this into a delicious supper. Try chicken breasts or salmon fillets lightly seasoned and scattered with lemon zest, for example.

Serves 4

4 medium-to-small sweet potatoes (about 600g), peeled
2 tbsp olive oil
¼ tsp sea salt
250g sour cream or crème fraîche to serve

for the chermoula:
1 tsp coriander seeds
1 tsp cumin seeds
50g coriander
50g flat-leaf parsley
1 tsp picked thyme leaves
1 garlic clove
2 tsp lemon zest
1 tbsp lemon juice
50ml extra virgin olive oil
½ tsp chilli flakes (plus extra to garnish)

Preheat the oven to 180°C/160°C fan. Cut the sweet potato into 4–5cm chunks and place on a baking tray. Toss the sweet potato in the oil and sprinkle with the salt then roast for 30 to 35 minutes, until it is tender and starting to crisp at the edges.

For the chermoula, toast the coriander and cumin seeds over a medium heat in a dry frying pan until they start to crackle and become fragrant. Add these to a food processor along with the coriander, parsley, thyme, garlic, lemon zest and juice, oil and chilli flakes and blitz until combined.

Spoon the chermoula over the sweet roasties and top with a dollop of sour cream or crème fraîche and a light sprinkling of chilli flakes.

Classic Caesar with Parmesan Shards

The trick here is to dry your lettuce well after you've washed it and to dress the croutons at the same time as the leaves. The croutons should be delicious little magnets for the Parmesan. It's worth using a microplane, which produces light snowflakes of Parmesan, rather than an old-school grater.

Serves 4

2 cos lettuces, trimmed and cut into quarters lengthways, or 4 baby gems cut in half
1 quantity Croutons (p.137)
50g freshly grated Parmesan
1 quantity Parmesan Shards (p.137)
salt and freshly ground black pepper

for the dressing:
1 tsp Dijon mustard
juice of ½ lemon
1 garlic clove, minced
30ml extra virgin olive oil
½ quantity Mayonnaise (p.136) or 200g good-quality shop-bought mayo
2 anchovy fillets, mashed to a paste (optional)

Make the dressing by whisking the mustard, lemon, garlic and oil into the mayo and, when combined, add the anchovies, if using. Taste and add salt and freshly ground black pepper to your liking.

Dress the lettuce and croutons in a wide shallow bowl, using your hands to make sure everything is well coated. Transfer to a serving plate and scatter over the freshly grated Parmesan then arrange the Parmesan shards. Add a final twist of black pepper before serving.

Spice-roasted Carrots

Roasting sweetens the carrots, and the spices make them super delicious. I like to use the multicoloured carrots you get at the beginning of the year in this salad if I can find them. There's no real difference in flavour; they just look beautiful.

Serves 4

500g carrots, scrubbed and
  sliced on a long diagonal
3 tbsp extra virgin olive oil
1 tbsp maple syrup
1 tsp smoked paprika
1 tsp ground cumin
1 tsp whole coriander seeds
¼ tsp ground ginger
¼ tsp ground cinnamon
¼ tsp ground turmeric
⅛ tsp cayenne
¼ tsp sea salt

for the dollop:
300g Greek yoghurt
25g coriander, finely
  chopped
zest and juice of ½ lime

Preheat the oven to 180°C/160°C fan. In a large bowl, mix the carrots, oil, maple syrup and all the spices and salt together, then tip them into a roasting tray lined with baking paper.

Roast for 25 to 30 minutes, or until the carrots are tender and starting to caramelise at the edges.

Whilst the carrots are roasting, make the dollop by mixing the yoghurt, coriander and lime zest and juice together. Serve the carrots warm with a tablespoon of the dollop on the side.

Celeriac Remoulade

Lemon and crème fraîche add a tang to this delicious wintery salad. Add the celeriac straight to the dressing as you chop it as it browns quickly.

Serves 4

juice of 1 lemon

3 tbsp good-quality mayonnaise or vegenaise

3 tbsp crème fraîche (omit if you're vegan and double the vegenaise)

1 tbsp wholegrain Dijon mustard

1 small-to-medium celeriac (about 700g), scrubbed

15g picked tarragon leaves, finely chopped

15g picked parsley leaves, finely chopped

2 tbsp tiny capers, rinsed

salt and freshly ground black pepper

First make the dressing by mixing the lemon juice, mayo, crème fraîche, mustard and black pepper to taste in a large bowl. Set aside.

Using a sharp knife, top and tail the celeriac, then stand it on one end and, following its curve, cut downward to remove the skin and nobbly bits.

Halve the celeriac and slice each half very thinly (use a mandoline, if you have one). Then, taking two or three slices at a time, chop the slices into matchsticks. When you get into a rhythm, the chopping action and seeing the results become pleasingly meditative.

Mix the dressing into the celeriac together with the tarragon, parsley and capers. Taste for seasoning and eat within 3 days.

The word February comes from the Latin *Februa* which means to cleanse and, without ever knowing that, I've always felt like sweeping out the dark corners of everything in February. It's a time for swapping tired old habits for sparks of energy and seeking out ways of getting whole grains and fresh veg in everything I can.

February

Roasted Baby Leeks with Romesco

Grilled calcot onions with romesco are a Catalan delicacy but here sweet baby leeks make a delicious alternative. I could eat them all day long but, truly, any roasted vegetable is delicious served with romesco.

Serves 4

12–15 baby leeks (approx. 350g)
3 tbsp extra virgin olive oil
2 garlic cloves, finely sliced
1 tbsp sherry vinegar or balsamic
1 tsp picked rosemary leaves, chopped
sea salt and freshly ground black pepper

for the romesco:
250g roasted red peppers from a jar or 1 quantity Roasted Peppers (p.138)
1 garlic clove, finely chopped
100g almonds, whole or flaked
100ml extra virgin olive oil
30ml red wine or sherry vinegar
1 tsp smoked paprika
½ tsp cayenne pepper
¼ tsp sea salt
50g breadcrumbs

Preheat the oven to 200°C/180°C fan. Make the romesco by pulsing the peppers, garlic, almonds, oil, vinegar, smoked paprika, cayenne pepper, salt and breadcrumbs together in a food processor or with a stick blender until everything is combined but still has texture.

Wash and trim the baby leeks and remove any tough or raggedy outer leaves. Bring a large pan of salted water to the boil, add the leeks and cook for 2 minutes to tenderise them. Then drain the leeks, slice them in half lengthways and pat dry.

Arrange the leeks in a roasting dish, add the oil and garlic and use your hands to make sure the leeks are well coated. Season and roast in the oven for about 8 minutes, or until golden brown and just beginning to crisp at the edges.

Transfer the leeks to a platter, along with the olive oily juices, add the sherry vinegar and sprinkle over the rosemary. Finally, spoon over the romesco and serve.

February

Cauliflower Tabbouleh

Here's a light twist on a classic salad where the herbs act as the fresh greens. The grapes are a slightly unconventional addition but they add a fresh, sweet pop I really like. You could easily swap the cauliflower for cooked bulgur wheat if you prefer.

Serves 4

1 medium cauliflower
(approx. 800g), trimmed

2 tbsp extra virgin olive oil

75g flat-leaf parsley

25g picked mint leaves

200g green seedless
grapes, halved

4 spring onions, finely
chopped

a decent glug (approx. 50ml)
extra virgin olive oil

juice of 1 lemon

1 garlic clove, grated

½ tsp sumac

sea salt and freshly ground
black pepper

Cut the cauliflower into florets and finely slice the core. For best results use a food processor and give four 2-second pulses to break the cauliflower down into a loose crumb-like texture. Or grate the cauliflower using the coarse side of a box grater – it takes more time, but the results will be just as good.

Heat the oil in a frying pan and sauté the cauliflower on a medium-to-low heat for about 5 minutes. You don't want to brown it, just soften it slightly. Transfer it to a large serving bowl and allow it to cool.

Next add the parsley and mint to the food processor and blitz in six 3-second blasts, pushing unchopped herbs down the side of the bowl between blasts if necessary. Again, elbow grease and a knife are a perfectly good replacement for a food processor here.

Stir the chopped herbs into the cauliflower along with the grapes and spring onions, then add the oil, lemon juice and garlic. Stir again so that everything is evenly integrated and season to taste. Finally, garnish with the sumac and serve.

Roasted Mushrooms with Spelt, Walnuts and Spicy Greens

If you don't have any spelt in the house, farro, pearl barley and bulgur wheat are all excellent substitutes. Dressing the grains while still warm helps them absorb flavour better and become more tender.

Serves 4

6 tbsp olive oil
250g spelt
250g chestnut mushrooms, brushed and sliced
75g butter, melted
150g walnut pieces
150g spicy greens such as rocket, mustard leaves or nasturtium leaves
3 tbsp lemon juice
1 tsp chopped thyme
sea salt and freshly ground black pepper

Preheat the oven to 220°C/200°C fan. Heat 2 tablespoons of the oil in a sauté pan. Add the spelt and mix so the oil coats each grain then cook over a medium heat for about 5 minutes. When you start to smell the toasted grains, add a big pinch of salt and enough water to cover the spelt by about 5cm, approximately 750ml. Bring to a boil, then reduce the heat and simmer uncovered for 25 minutes, or for the time specified on the packet. When done, the grains should be chewy and tender. Drain whatever liquid is left and allow to cool.

While the spelt is cooking, toss the mushrooms in the melted butter and arrange in a single layer on a baking tray lined with greaseproof paper. Roast for 10 minutes, then add the walnut pieces and roast together for a further 5 minutes, until everything is golden and beginning to crisp. Season well.

Roughly chop the greens and add these to the spelt in a large bowl. Whisk together the lemon juice with the remaining 4 tablespoons of oil and the thyme, then add to the spelt and greens and toss to combine. Add the mushrooms and walnuts whilst still warm and serve.

Crispy Leek and Barley Salad with Jammy Eggs and Thyme

I love the melt-in-your-mouth, candy-floss-like consistency of leeks cooked this way. They can be made a day in advance and stored in an airtight container and are delicious on everything, including cheese on toast.

Serves 4

200g pearl barley, rinsed
1 leek, white and pale green part only
200ml sunflower oil
¼ tsp sea salt
¼ tsp cayenne pepper
4 free-range Jammy Eggs (p.139), peeled and halved
sea salt and freshly ground black pepper to taste

for the dressing:
2 tbsp extra virgin olive oil
2 tbsp red wine vinegar
1 shallot, minced
1 tbsp wholegrain mustard
1 tsp rosemary, finely chopped
1 tbsp fresh thyme, finely chopped

Cover the barley with cold water in a large pan, bring to the boil and simmer for about 30 minutes, until tender, then drain well to prevent sogginess.

Cut the leek in half lengthways, then slice lengthways again into fine even strips about 1–2mm wide. Heat the oil in a smallish pan and fry the leek in four batches until golden. Pile the tangled strands in a bowl lined with kitchen paper to absorb the oil and season with the salt and cayenne pepper.

To make the dressing, whisk the oil, vinegar, shallot, mustard and rosemary together and stir a tablespoon at a time into the warm barley until the grains are lightly coated. Fold in the thyme.

Transfer the dressed barley to a serving plate and top with the crispy leeks and the halved eggs. Season with salt and a twist or five of freshly ground black pepper and serve.

February

Green shoots, days getting lighter and a little longer and the warmth of the first sunshine on your shoulders. Fresh, peppery watercress starts to appear and so does newly made goat's cheese with its almost lemony tang. The energy of the dawn chorus tells you that spring is here.

March

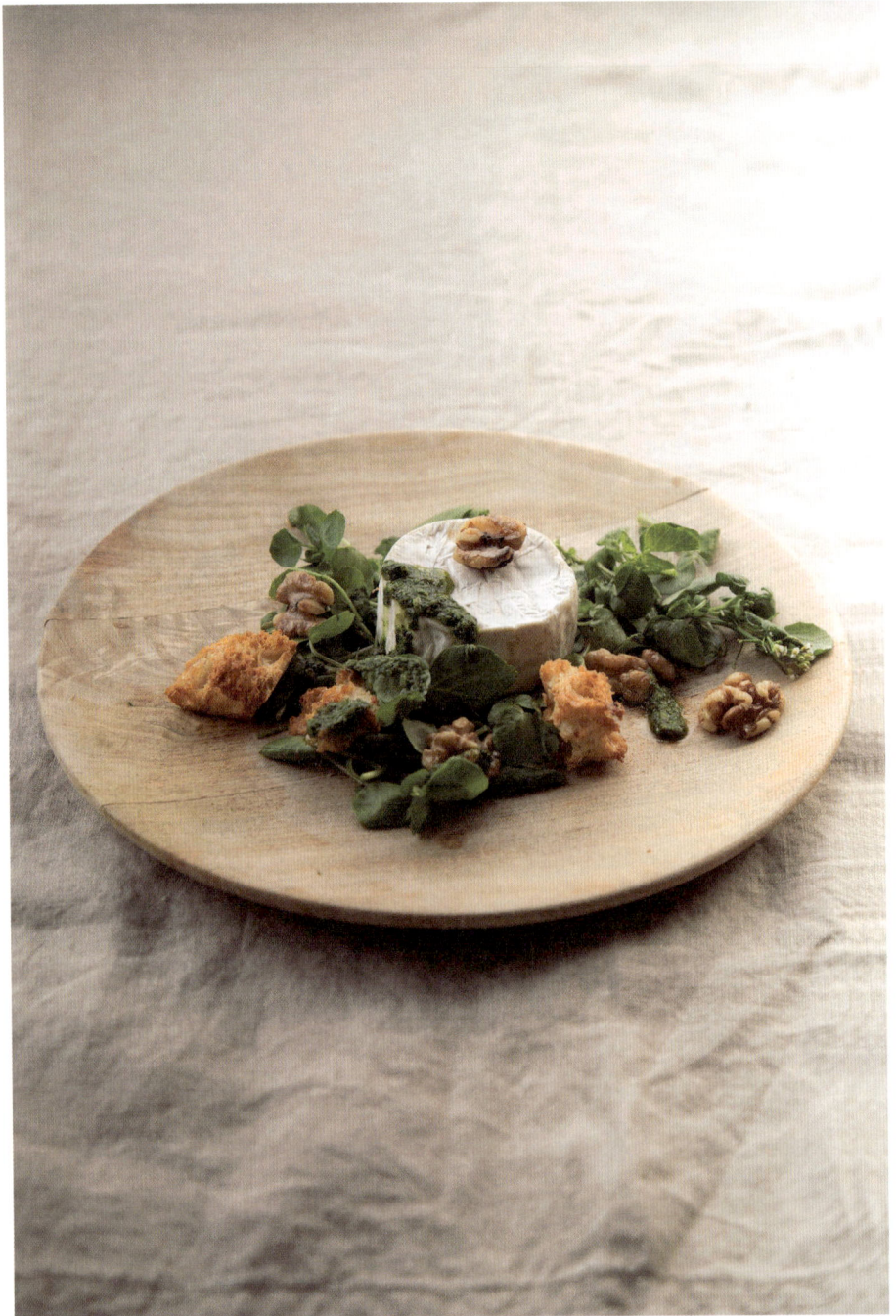

Goat's Cheese and Salsa Verde

Fresh goat's cheese straight from the maker is really worth seeking out in spring – try your local cheese shop or a good cheese counter. Peppery watercress is beautiful in this salad but it fades quickly once picked. Store it in the fridge in a bowl of water with a slice of lemon in it to keep it crisp.

Serves 4

3 slices of stale bread cut into bite-sized cubes
150g shelled walnuts
50ml extra virgin olive oil
1 garlic clove, crushed
25g butter
200g watercress, baby spinach, oak leaf or a mix
250g goat's cheese log sliced into 4, or 4 buttons such as Crottin or Capricorn
sea salt and freshly ground black pepper

for the salsa verde:
25g picked flat-leaf parsley leaves
25g picked basil leaves
10g picked tarragon leaves
1 tbsp capers, rinsed and patted dry
1 small shallot, finely minced
120ml extra virgin olive oil
40ml sherry vinegar
2 anchovy fillets (optional)

Preheat the oven to 200°C /180°C fan. On a baking tray, toss the bread and walnuts with the oil and garlic, then season with ¼ teaspoon of salt and dot on the butter. Bake in the oven for 10 to 15 minutes, giving an occasional shoogle so that nothing burns. Set aside to cool while you make the salsa verde.

Blitz the parsley, basil, tarragon, capers, shallot, oil, vinegar and anchovies, if using, in a food processor using 2- to 3-second pulses, or carefully grind everything in a mortar and pestle. The different methods will yield different textures of sauce, but both are equally good.

Arrange the leaves and goat's cheese on a serving plate and scatter over the croutons and walnuts. Then drizzle over the salsa verde, season to taste and serve.

Roasted Peppers, Orzo and Manchego

I always double the quantity of roasted peppers and store the extra when I make this. That way I have them customised the way I like, with extra garlic and rosemary, for loads of other dishes. If you're in a hurry, shop-bought roasted peppers are a good, quick alternative.

Serves 4

750ml vegetable stock
250g orzo
1 quantity Roasted Peppers (p.138) or 250g shop-bought roasted peppers
2 tbsp extra virgin olive oil
3 garlic cloves, thinly sliced
1 tsp fennel seeds
1 tsp coriander seeds
1 tsp paprika
2 tbsp red wine vinegar or sherry vinegar
2–3 sprigs rosemary or thyme, finely chopped
25g picked basil leaves
25g rocket
100g Manchego, shaved in thin slices from the block

In a pan over a medium heat, bring the stock to a simmer, add the orzo, bring back to a simmer and cook for 10 to 12 minutes (or according to the packet instructions), until tender. Drain, reserving 50ml (roughly 3 tablespoons) of the stock, and set aside to cool.

Cut the peppers into finger-width strips. Then, in a large sauté pan, heat the oil over a medium heat, add the garlic and swirl for a minute or two until it softens. Add the fennel and coriander seeds and paprika and cook for another minute or so, until the fennel is fragrant. Remove the pan from the heat, add the orzo and the reserved stock and mix until everything is well coated. Add the peppers, vinegar and rosemary or thyme, mix and transfer to a serving dish. Just before serving, scatter over the basil, rocket and thin shavings of Manchego.

March

Spiced Paneer with Coriander and Lime Salad

I make this salad with paneer because we love it so much in our house, but it would be just as delicious with grilled chicken or king prawns in its place.

Serves 4

225g paneer, cut into 2cm
  cubes
1 tsp garam masala
¼ tsp salt
1 tbsp sunflower or rapeseed
  oil

for the salad:
juice of 2 limes
1 tbsp olive oil
½ tsp ground coriander
1 red serrano chilli, deseeded
  and finely diced
1 cucumber, peeled, halved
  lengthways, deseeded and
  thinly sliced
1 red onion, halved and thinly
  sliced
50g fresh coriander, stems
  finely chopped, leaves
  roughly chopped
25g picked mint leaves,
  roughly chopped
75g roasted peanuts,
  chopped

Toss the cubes of paneer in a large bowl with the garam masala and the salt.

Heat the sunflower oil in a large frying pan over a medium heat and fry the paneer for 2 to 3 minutes on each side until crisp and golden then set aside.

Whisk the lime juice, olive oil, ground coriander and chilli together in a bowl large enough to hold the salad, then add the cucumber, red onion, fresh coriander and mint. Using two forks or your clean hands, toss everything together until it is well dressed, then transfer it to a serving plate and add the paneer. Finally, scatter over the chopped peanuts and serve.

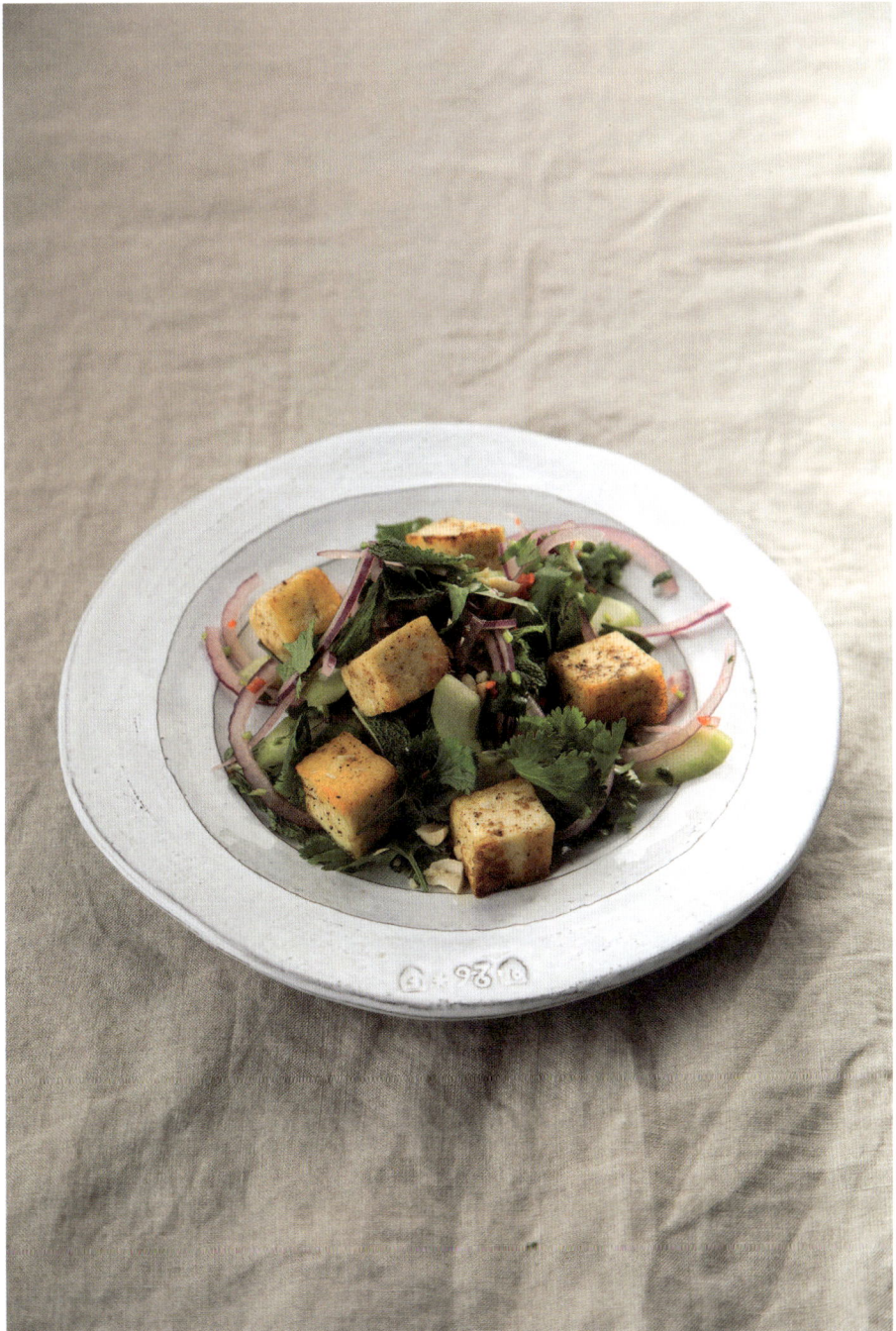

Emerald Divinity

This green, intensely delicious dressing is perfect poured on crisp flavour vessels like celery and baby gem leaves. Or dip crisps in it. Try it on grilled chicken or over crispy tofu. It's the taste of spring in a sauce. For a healthier alternative, replace the mayonnaise with one very ripe avocado.

Serves 4

4 baby gem lettuces, cut lengthwise into quarters

4 celery sticks, tough strings removed, sliced

1 small fennel bulb, thinly sliced

4 spring onions, trimmed and thinly sliced

for the dressing:

50g picked flat-leaf parsley leaves

50g watercress, tough stems removed

2 tbsp picked tarragon leaves

10g picked basil leaves

3 tbsp fresh lemon juice

1 tbsp white wine vinegar

50ml olive oil

100g mayonnaise or vegenaise

¼ tsp sea salt

Make the dressing by blitzing the parsley, watercress, tarragon and basil in a blender for two 10-second pulses, then add the lemon juice, vinegar, oil, mayonnaise or vegenaise and the salt and blend until incorporated.

Arrange the lettuce, celery, fennel and spring onions on a large platter. Either serve the dressing on the side so people can add their own or dip, or drizzle the dressing over.

36

Seared Hispi with Cherries and Smoked Almonds

Take care to keep all the leaves attached to the base when you're preparing the cabbage. And even though they're a little more expensive, it's worth seeking out real smoked almonds rather than smoke-flavoured ones. The light smoky flavour works so well with the cherries; it's a total treat.

Serves 4

2 small hispi or sweetheart cabbages, trimmed and tough outer leaves removed
2 tbsp sunflower oil

for the dressing:
70ml extra virgin olive oil
25ml cider vinegar
25ml maple syrup
1 tbsp wholegrain Dijon mustard
150g smoked almonds, chopped
150g dried cherries, chopped

Make the dressing by whisking the oil, vinegar, maple syrup and mustard together, then stir in the almonds and cherries. Set aside and let the cherries swell a bit in the dressing.

Bring a large pan of salted water to the boil. Cut the cabbages lengthwise into quarters and blanche them for 1 to 2 minutes, then drain.

Rub each of the cabbage quarters with the sunflower oil and, in a very hot frying pan or skillet, sear them for 2 to 3 minutes on each side. Aim for some very satisfactory charring but not actual burning.

Arrange the cabbage on a plate, drizzle over the dressing and serve.

This is the month of light mornings and lighter evenings. We see the prettiness of blossoms on the trees before they settle down to the business of coming into leaf and then fruit – a relief, at last, from the darkness of winter. Easter and spring holidays bring packed picnics and family feasts, celebrating with comforting warm lentils and fresh zingy salads.

April

Vietnamese Carrot Salad

This is one of my favourite salads ever. Vegetarian fish sauce is available in many larger supermarkets and online and it's pretty good. Crispy Shallots (see p.138) are a delicious addition to this, and grilled chicken or prawns go perfectly with it too.

Serves 4

400–500g Chinese cabbage
250g carrots, peeled
75g pink radishes or mooli (daikon)
2 small shallots, peeled
100g beansprouts
50g picked mint leaves
50g coriander, roughly chopped with stems
25g picked Thai basil leaves or basil leaves
75g salted peanuts, roughly chopped

for the dressing:
juice of 3 limes
1 red serrano chilli, deseeded and finely sliced
1 garlic clove, grated
3 tbsp nam pla fish sauce (or vegetarian alternative)
1 tbsp sesame oil
1 tsp soft brown sugar

In a large bowl, make the dressing by mixing the lime juice, chilli, garlic, nam pla, oil and brown sugar. Stir until the sugar is dissolved.

Finely chop the cabbage and either grate the carrots or cut them into long thin matchsticks and add them to the dressing. Finely slice the radishes and shallots into thin discs and add them to the dressing along with the beansprouts. Mix well, and just before serving fold in the mint and coriander and finish by sprinkling over the basil and chopped peanuts.

Kale Ultra

This salad is all about the dressing. Massaging it into the kale makes the leaves super tender and the seeds give it crunch. You've got to love something that makes kale, one of the most nutritionally dense foods on earth, deliciously moreish.

Serves 4

200g kale (Russian, curly,
    cavolo nero or a mix)
80g baby spinach
2 tbsp sunflower seeds
2 tbsp pumpkin seeds
2 tbsp linseeds

for the dressing:
20g baby spinach
2 picked lime leaves
juice of ½ lemon
juice of 1 lime
50ml cloudy apple juice
20g fresh ginger, grated
1 kiwi fruit, peeled
1 green chilli, deseeded
50ml extra virgin olive oil
1 tbsp maple syrup

Wash and dry the kale well. Remove and discard the tough stems, then tear the leaves into bite-sized pieces and arrange in a large bowl with the 80g of spinach.

Make the dressing by blitzing the 20g of spinach, lime leaves, lemon and lime juices, apple juice, ginger, kiwi, chilli, oil and maple syrup in a food processor. Fold the dressing into the kale and use your hands to massage it into the leaves.

Toast the seeds in a dry frying pan until they start to snap and pop a little and become shiny, about 2 minutes. Scatter the seeds over the dressed salad and serve.

Green Lentils with Velvety Onions and Oregano Mojo

This mojo is a version of one served at the amazing Terre à Terre restaurant in Brighton. It's a flash of neon green that illuminates the earthy lentils, and it's fantastic on everything from omelettes to quesadillas.

Serves 4

400g Puy lentils
2 bay leaves
1 quantity Velvety Onions (p.139)
1 tbsp red wine vinegar
sea salt and freshly ground black pepper

for the oregano mojo:
25g picked oregano leaves
25g picked flat-leaf parsley leaves
½ green serrano chilli, deseeded
juice of ½ lime
¼ tsp sea salt
150ml extra virgin olive oil

Put the lentils and bay leaves in a medium pan and cover by at least 3–4 cm of cold water. Bring to a boil, then turn the heat down and simmer until tender, 20 to 25 minutes.

Make the oregano mojo by blitzing the oregano, parsley, chilli, lime, salt and oil in a food processor or with a stick blender, then set aside.

When the lentils are just tender (you don't want them to be mushy), drain and remove the bay leaves. Return them to the pan and fold in the onions, with all their juices, then season and add the red wine vinegar to make a sort of instant dressing. Finally, transfer to a serving dish, spoon the mojo over the top and serve.

Super Green Tahini Quinoa
– give yourself a fighting chance!

Quinoa is one of the kitchen good guys. You can cook it in big batches and refrigerate or freeze the cooked grain so it's there when you need it, and it's rich in protein, fibre and B vitamins. Most quinoa is pre-rinsed so there's no need to worry about that step unless the packet instructions tell you to do it.

Serves 4

200g red or white quinoa, rinsed unless otherwise stated on packet
½ tsp sea salt
1 × 400g tin chickpeas, drained and rinsed
100g pumpkin seeds
100g sunflower seeds
200g sugar snap peas, halved on the diagonal
50g pea shoots

for the dressing:
2 garlic cloves, crushed
50g rocket
25g picked mint leaves
15g picked flat-leaf parsley leaves
70g light tahini
juice and zest of 1 lemon
2 tbsp olive oil
sea salt and freshly ground black pepper

Add the quinoa to a medium saucepan with 375ml of water, bring to a boil then turn down to simmer, covered, for about 15 minutes or until the water has evaporated and you can see a little white tail on each grain. Set aside to cool and let the grains fluff for 5 minutes, then sprinkle in the sea salt and fork through.

Make the dressing by blitzing the garlic, rocket, mint, parsley, tahini, lemon juice and zest, oil and 2 tablespoons of water with a stick blender (or mash with a mortar and pestle) until well incorporated. Taste and season to your liking.

Add the chickpeas, seeds and sugar snaps to the quinoa and toss in the chlorophyl-intense dressing. Transfer to a serving bowl and sprinke over the pea shoots before serving.

The woods are full of bluebells and starry white wild garlic flowers. Leave the bluebells and pick just as much wild garlic as you can eat. Days are fresh and warm in the sun, after the cool, blue, still early mornings. Windowsill plants yield tender little leaves and this month's papery-skinned new potatoes are so worth a celebration feast.

May

New Potato Salad with Wild Garlic Mayonnaise

If you're out picking your own wild garlic, be sure to wash it really well. Use the white star-like flowers to garnish this salad if you can find them.

Serves 4

750g small new potatoes such as Ayrshire or Jersey Royals, skin on, cut into equal-sized pieces

zest and juice of 1 lemon

1 red onion, halved and finely sliced

25g picked flat-leaf parsley leaves, roughly chopped

50g baby kale, picked from thick stems

25g lovage or celery leaves, chopped

4 celery stalks, tough strings removed, thinly sliced

100g small cornichons, roughly chopped (optional)

salt

for the wild garlic mayo:

150g mayonnaise or vegenaise

50g wild garlic, washed and dried

pinch of sea salt

30ml extra virgin olive oil

Boil the potatoes in salted water until tender, about 12 to 15 minutes.

In a large bowl, mix the lemon zest and juice together with the sliced red onion.

Then make the wild garlic mayonnaise. In a mortar and pestle, mash the wild garlic leaves, salt and oil until puréed to a pulp and mix this into the mayonnaise. Chill until needed.

Drain the potatoes and set them aside to cool. Add the parsley, kale, lovage or celery leaves, celery and cornichons, if using, to the onion in the large bowl.

In a separate bowl, mix the cooled boiled potatoes with the wild garlic mayonnaise then transfer to a serving dish. Scatter the salad over the potatoes and serve.

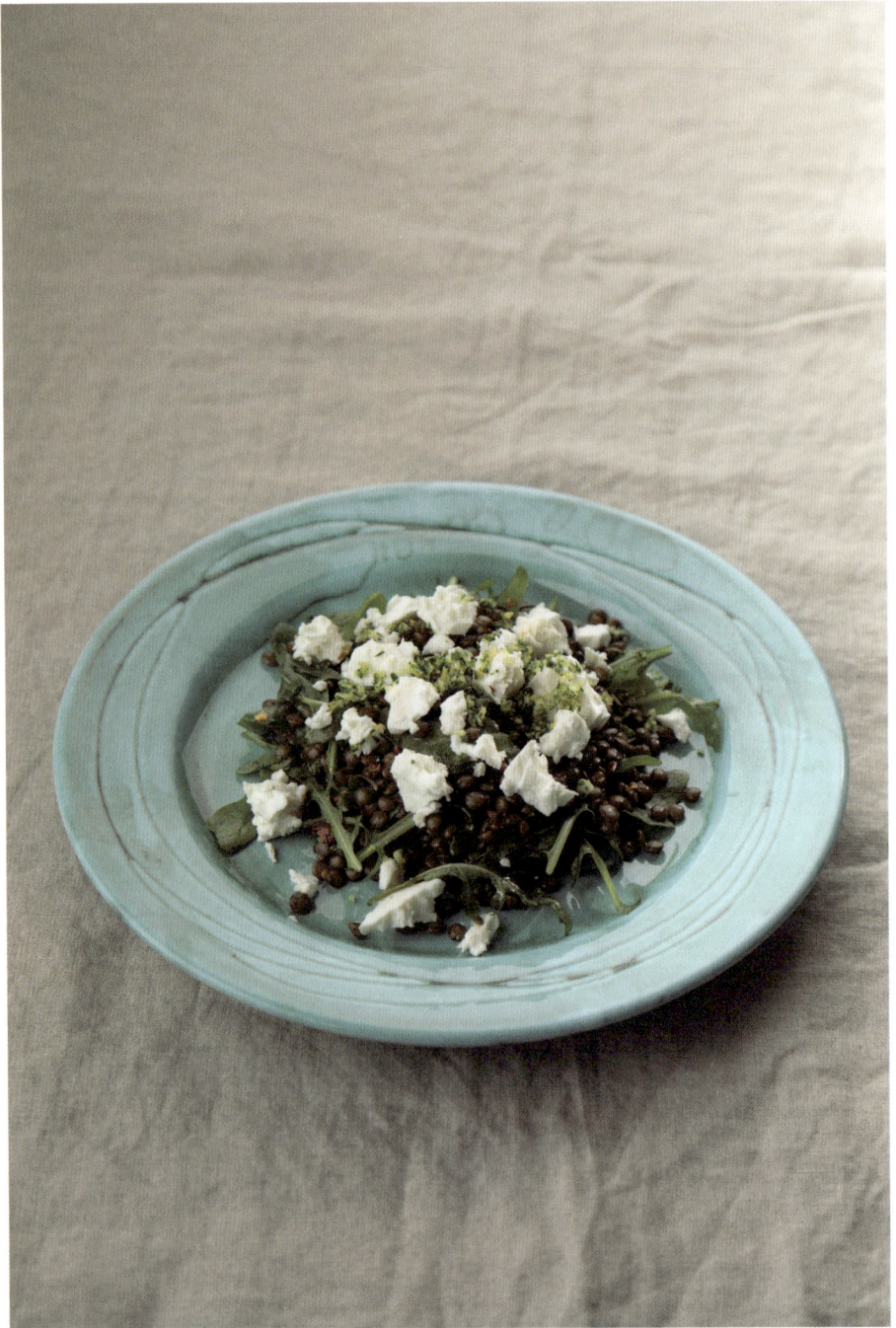

Puy Lentils with Feta and Sorrel Gremolata

Traditionally gremolata is made by chopping together parsley, lemon zest and garlic, but I couldn't resist adding sorrel for some extra tang – it just makes this salad vibrate with spring-y energy. Once you've learnt to spot sorrel in the wild, you'll be amazed by how prevalent it is.

Serves 4

250g Puy lentils
3 garlic cloves, smashed
3 sprigs fresh thyme
100g mizuna or rocket
200g feta
sea salt

for the dressing:
60ml extra virgin olive oil
45ml sherry vinegar
1 tsp red chilli flakes

for the gremolata:
20g picked sorrel leaves
15g picked flat-leaf parsley leaves
1 garlic clove, finely grated or chopped
zest of ½ lemon

Rinse the lentils and put them in a pan with plenty of cold water, the garlic and thyme and bring it to a simmer. Cook for 20 to 25 minutes, until the lentils are tender but still firm.

While the lentils cook, make the dressing by whisking together the oil, vinegar and chilli flakes in a large serving bowl.

Make the gremolata by finely chopping the sorrel and parsley together and then chopping in the garlic and the lemon zest.

When the lentils are ready, drain them well, remove the thyme, then stir the lentils into the dressing. Warm lentils absorb dressing better. Once cooled, fold in the mizuna or rocket and crumble over the feta in decent-sized pieces. Finally, sprinkle over the gremolata, taste and season with salt if it needs it and serve.

Asparagus and Radishes
with Pink Grapefruit Vinaigrette

There's something doubly delicious about searing
asparagus in olive oil until it starts to char. It makes it
sweet and keeps it crisp – and it's fast as anything.

Serves 4

2 bunches asparagus
(approx. 600g), woody
ends trimmed

200g pink radishes
(preferably with leaves
attached), sliced into discs

2 tbsp extra virgin olive oil

the smaller leaves from
the radish bunch or 150g
mustard leaves, washed
and dried

1 pink grapefruit, peel cut off
and segments cut out (zest
and juice reserved for the
vinaigrette)

sea salt and freshly ground
black pepper

for the citrus vinaigrette:

1 medium shallot, finely
diced

2 tbsp white wine vinegar

60ml extra virgin olive oil

½ tsp grapefruit zest

50ml pink grapefruit juice

1 tsp maple syrup

pinch of sea salt

Mix the shallot and vinegar together in a small
bowl and set aside for at least half an hour.

Heat a heavy-based skillet until hot. Toss the
asparagus and radishes in the oil in a bowl and
season well. Sear the asparagus first, letting it
crackle and sizzle in the pan. It should go bright
green within about a minute, then turn the spears
over and cook them for a further minute or so
before removing them from the pan. Then add the
radishes to the pan, cooking until they become
translucent. When ready, set them aside with the
asparagus. Toss the leaves in the residual oil in
the pan and arrange on your serving plate. Then
add the seared asparagus and radishes and the
grapefruit segments.

Add the oil, grapefruit zest and juice, maple syrup
and the salt to the shallot mixture and whisk well.
Drizzle the dressing over the seared vegetables,
season and serve immediately.

Quick Pickled Carrots with Whipped Ricotta and Garlicky Breadcrumbs

Peppery nasturtium leaves can be hard to find in the shops but they're very easy to grow yourself on a windowsill or in a doorstep pot. If you can't find them, rocket is a good substitute. Any Quick Pickles (see p.139) you like could be substituted for the carrots here.

Serves 4

for the whipped ricotta:
250g ricotta
¼ tsp sea salt
1 tbsp extra virgin olive oil
10g picked basil leaves, chopped
10g chives, chopped

100g nasturtium leaves or rocket
2 tsp olive oil
150g vine tomatoes, chopped
50g green olives
150g quick pickled carrots (see Quick Pickles p.139)
1 quantity Garlicky Breadcrumbs (p.137) (optional)
sea salt

In a food processor or bowl with an electric whisk, briefly blend the ricotta and salt (just to combine them). Then, with the motor running, slowly drizzle in the oil, processing until the ricotta is smooth and creamy, about 2 minutes. Fold in the chopped basil and chives.

Toss the nasturtium leaves or rocket in the olive oil and a pinch of salt.

Spread the ricotta over the base of your serving plate, sprinkle over the dressed leaves then the tomatoes, olives and pickled carrots. Finally, sprinkle over the garlicky breadcrumbs, if using, and serve.

The start of summer and the shipping
forecast brings happy news of seeing
for miles and slow-moving high pressure.
Broad bean flowers have turned to pods
and courgettes, cherries, sorrel and
gooseberries are all there to inspire you.

June

Gazpacho Salad

Magic happens when fresh marjoram and ripe tomatoes get together! Serve this with lots of crusty country bread so you can mop up any leftover dressing when the salad is finished. And listen to Rodrigo y Gabriela playing 'Cumbé' when you're making it.

Serves 4

1kg very ripe plum tomatoes
1 red pepper
1 green pepper
1 cucumber
20g picked marjoram leaves, chopped
1 quantity Garlicky Breadcrumbs (p.137)
sea salt and freshly ground black pepper

for the dressing:
40ml sherry vinegar
100ml extra virgin olive oil

Chop the tomatoes into large bite-sized pieces. Halve and deseed the red and green peppers and chop them into pieces roughly the same size as the tomatoes. Peel the cucumber and chop it into similar-sized chunks.

Transfer the vegetables to a serving dish, then mix the vinegar and oil and dress the salad. Season the salad with salt and generous quantities of black pepper, then scatter the marjoram and breadcrumbs over the top and serve.

Courgettes with Hazelnuts and Pistou

How do you make this salad amazing? Caerphilly! This light, crumbly cheese works perfectly with the courgettes. Blanching the basil for the pistou seems like an extra layer of effort but it's worth it because it fixes the chlorophyl in the tender leaves and stops the pistou from becoming too dark.

Serves 4

3 medium courgettes

1 tangy apple such as Granny Smith or Cox's Orange Pippin

juice of ½ lemon

30ml extra virgin olive oil

50g hazelnuts

100g good-quality Caerphilly, Wensleydale or Bonnet cheese

sea salt and freshly ground black pepper

for the pistou:

50g basil leaves and stalks (a handful of leaves reserved and chopped to garnish)

2 garlic cloves, peeled and crushed

60ml extra virgin olive oil

¼ tsp sea salt

Using a vegetable peeler, slice the courgettes into pappardelle-style strips. Peel and cut the apple into equally thin pieces.

In a large serving bowl, whisk together the lemon juice and oil, and toss the courgette and apple in it.

Toast the hazelnuts in a dry frying pan for 2 to 3 minutes, until fragrant. Transfer them to a board, roughly chop them and sprinkle lightly with salt.

Now make the pistou. Blanche the basil for 10 seconds, refresh it in iced water then squeeze all the water from it. Use a stick blender, food processor or mortar and pestle to blend the basil, garlic, oil and salt.

Arrange the courgette and apple on a plate, dot with the pistou and sprinkle over the hazelnuts and chopped basil. Finally, shave over curls of cheese, season and serve.

New Potatoes with Samphire and Broad Beans

Samphire is naturally salty so taste the salad before you season it, and there's no need to peel new potatoes – the skins are thin and delicious. This is the perfect accompaniment to smoked salmon or halibut.

Serves 4

450g new potatoes, halved or cut so all a similar size
600g broad beans in their pods
100g samphire, trimmed
15g dill, thicker stems removed, roughly chopped
200g sweet cherry tomatoes on the vine, halved
salt and freshly ground black pepper

for the dressing:
1 tsp Dijon mustard
½ garlic clove, grated or finely chopped
1 tbsp red wine vinegar or cider vinegar
50ml extra virgin olive oil
sea salt and freshly ground black pepper

Put the potatoes in a pan of cold salted water, bring to a boil and simmer for 15 to 18 minutes, or until tender. For the last 5 minutes of cooking, steam the broad beans in a sieve or colander placed over the pan of simmering potatoes. When the beans are ready, set them aside to cool and drain the potatoes.

Make the dressing by whisking together the mustard, garlic, vinegar, oil and salt and pepper to taste in a large bowl, then add the warm potatoes and mix until they're well coated.

Shell the broad beans from their papery cases and add them to the potatoes along with the samphire, dill and tomatoes and bring together gently. Season the salad, then serve.

Globe Artichokes with Lemon Dressing

There's something gleefully wild about eating artichokes like this. Children love it and it really breaks down barriers if you're sharing with friends. Sleeves must be rolled up; hands are going to get dirty. Choose heavy-headed artichokes and keep them fresh by standing them stem-first in a vase of water like flowers, which, of course, they are.

Serves 4

4 medium globe artichokes
1 lemon
1 tsp sea salt
1 tsp Dijon mustard
4 tbsp Greek yoghurt, mayonnaise or vegenaise
1 clove garlic, grated
3 tbsp extra virgin olive oil

Fill a pot large enough to hold the artichokes and the lemon (left whole) with water and bring to a boil. Add the artichokes, lemon and salt, slap on the lid and bring back to a simmer for 25 to 30 minutes, until the base of the globe is tender enough to be easily pierced by the tip of a knife.

Drain the cooked artichokes stem side up on a wire rack over the sink until they're cool enough to touch then, using a sharp knife, cut off the stems to make a flat base for each globe.

To make the dressing, squeeze the warm juice from the poached lemon and whisk it into the mustard, yoghurt or mayo, garlic and oil, and divide this between four little serving bowls.

To eat the artichokes, pull the leaves out, dipping them into the dressing and scraping off the delicate meat with your teeth. Work your way until you get to the thistly fluff that guards the tender heart – tear that away and enjoy your prize.

This is perhaps the most delicious time of year. Festival season, picnic season and school holidays... all the best reasons for making fresh, delicious feasts that celebrate what's thriving in the garden and fresh from the fields. Tender leaves and herbs, greens and beans, berries, shoots and sweet roots like radishes.

July

Watermelon Salad with Lime Sherbet and Spiced Nuts

Put on 'Watermelon Sugar' by Harry Styles and make this fresh, tangy salad. Children might well give you deity status when they know you can make your own sherbet. It's not difficult to get hold of the citric acid needed to make it – you can find it online or in a chemist. Or swap in a yellow sherbet fountain!

Serves 4

1 red onion, finely sliced

juice of 2 limes (use the zest for the lime sherbet)

1.5kg watermelon (half an average-sized one), peeled and chopped into 5cm cubes

1 tbsp extra virgin olive oil

25g coriander, stems chopped finely, leaves chopped roughly

1 quantity Spiced Nuts (p.138)

for the lime sherbet:

zest of 2 limes

20g picked mint leaves

½ tsp citric acid

50g caster sugar

Place the sliced red onion in a small dish, cover with the lime juice and leave to macerate for at least 15 minutes, until the onions are neon pink.

Make the lime sherbet by putting the lime zest, mint, citric acid and sugar on a clean chopping board and chopping all together until it becomes a fine powder.

Put the melon pieces in a serving dish and scatter over the onion along with the lime juice, then drizzle over the oil and sprinkle over the coriander.

Serve the watermelon salad with the lime sherbet and spiced nuts on the side so people can help themselves as they like.

Jewelled Rice Salad

Cherries taste so amazing in this salad that I make sure to buy frozen fresh ones when they're no longer in season and difficult to find in the shops. That way I never run out.

Serves 4

250g brown rice, rinsed well
½ tsp salt
50g butter
4–5 saffron strands
100g fresh cherries, pitted and halved
100g pomegranate seeds, 25g reserved to garnish
100g dried cranberries
50g shelled pistachios
50g dried apricots, chopped
zest and juice of ½ orange
½ tsp cinnamon
1 small bunch spring onions, trimmed and finely chopped
20g picked mint or flat-leaf parsley leaves, finely chopped, a handful reserved to garnish

for the dressing:
50ml pomegranate molasses
50ml extra virgin olive oil
25ml lemon juice
1 clove garlic, grated
sea salt and freshly ground black pepper

Put the rice in a saucepan with 500ml water and the salt, butter and saffron and simmer, covered, for 40 minutes. When done, turn off the heat and leave to steam with the lid on for 10 minutes before transferring to a large bowl and fluffing with a fork.

When the rice has cooled a little, add the cherries, pomegranate seeds, cranberries, pistachios, apricots, orange zest and juice, cinnamon, spring onions and mint or parsley.

Make the dressing by combining the pomegranate molasses, oil, lemon juice and garlic and gently mix this through the rice. Check and correct the seasoning if it needs it.

Transfer to a serving dish and garnish with the reserved pomegranate seeds and herbs.

Classic Fattoush

Sumac is the cornerstone of this traditional Middle Eastern bread salad. Don't be tempted to substitute as it's got this incredibly distinctive sour, lemony flavour.

Serves 4

3 wholewheat pitta breads
250g sweet cherry tomatoes
1 cucumber
1 cos lettuce, chopped
8 radishes, thinly sliced
25g picked mint leaves
25g picked flat-leaf parsley
  leaves
2 spring onions, trimmed
  and chopped
100g purslane (optional)

for the dressing:
70ml extra virgin olive oil
2 tbsp pomegranate
  molasses
2 tbsp sumac
juice of ½ lemon
¼ tsp salt

Preheat the grill to medium.

Make the dressing by whisking together the oil, pomegranate molasses, sumac, lemon juice and salt, and brush it on one side of each pitta (or use your fingertips), reserving the leftover dressing. Grill the pitta (on the dressed side) until they are golden and crisp, then set aside.

Halve the cherry tomatoes and add them to a large serving bowl. Peel the cucumber, halve it lengthways and deseed it using a teaspoon, then chop it into even-sized chunks and throw them in with the tomatoes. Add the lettuce, radishes, mint, parsley, spring onions and purslane, if using, to the bowl. Then crumble over the pitta bread in rough pieces. Dress the salad with the remaining dressing and mix gently but well before serving.

Greek Salad

In Greece, it's traditional to serve the feta in one big piece with the dressed tomato salad around it. If you want to serve it like that, dress the feta with a decent splash of olive oil and a scattering of lemon zest and chopped marjoram. Whatever way you serve it, warm bread to soak up the juices and dressing is essential.

Serves 4

1 red onion, sliced very thinly
juice of ½ lemon (25ml)
800g very ripe plum tomatoes on the vine
1 cucumber
2 red peppers
200g pitted Kalamata olives
5–6 sprigs of fresh marjoram or oregano, leaves picked and chopped
200g good-quality Greek feta, cut into large cubes
sea salt and freshly ground black pepper

for the dressing:
75ml extra virgin olive oil
30ml red wine vinegar
1 clove garlic, finely grated
¼ tsp sea salt

Put the sliced red onion in a small bowl with the lemon juice and set aside while you prepare everything else.

Halve the tomatoes, then cut the halves into chunky quarters and season with a pinch of salt.

Peel the cucumber, halve it lengthways then cut it into pieces roughly the same size as the tomatoes. Deseed the peppers and cut them into similar-sized chunks.

Gently mix the onion, tomatoes, cucumber, peppers, olives and marjoram or oregano on a serving plate.

Make the dressing by whisking together the oil, vinegar, garlic and salt, and pour it over the salad. Scatter over the feta, then season with salt and lots of freshly ground black pepper and serve.

Grilled Halloumi, Pineapple and Pak Choi

This is a fresh, tangy zinger of a salad made a little mellow by grilling the pineapple, which softens the flavour, and by adding a little hemp oil. Take care to sear the pak choi and not cook it through – it should still have a pleasing crunch.

Serves 4

8 baby pak choi or 3 large ones
½ medium pineapple, skin cut off
225g good-quality halloumi, sliced
2 tbsp extra virgin olive oil
20g coriander, roughly chopped
20g picked mint leaves, torn or chopped

for the dressing:
zest and juice of 1 lime
2 tbsp fresh pineapple juice
4cm piece of fresh ginger, grated
2 tbsp hemp oil

Trim the bottoms of the pak choi, leaving the leaves attached, then cut in half (or in quarters if they are larger). Cut the pineapple in half then into slices roughly 1.5cm thick, making sure to save any juice for the salad dressing. Cut the halloumi into slices the same thickness as the pineapple and pat them dry.

Make the dressing by whisking together the lime zest and juice, pineapple juice, ginger and hemp oil – or shake it up in a jar.

Heat a ribbed grill pan, sauté pan or barbecue to very hot and grill the pak choi, pineapple then halloumi, brushing each item with oil before you cook it – about two minutes on the first side and one on the second should do it. You are looking for nicely caramelised surfaces. Lay the grilled ingredients on a platter as you cook them. When everything is assembled, drizzle over the dressing, scatter over the coriander and mint and serve.

This is deep summer: barbecues, coastal exploration, bare feet and lazing in the shade of trees. Strawberries and creamy burrata make a magnificent centrepiece to a family dinner. Spicy noodles full of crunchy greens, and couscous with sweet juicy mangos make excellent portable feasts.

August

Spinach Salad with Strawberries and Burrata

This is pretty much my perfect summer salad. Burrata, a type of mozzarella, has soft creamy curds in the middle, which is why it is not cut up before it goes into the salad. Freshly ground black pepper and sweet strawberries is one of those surprising culinary relationships that become a happy revelation when first tasted.

Serves 4

250g strawberries
70g rocket
70g baby spinach
25g picked basil leaves
4 × 125g burrata
salt and freshly ground black
  pepper

for the dressing:
3 tbsp extra virgin olive oil
3 tbsp fresh lemon juice
1 tsp maple syrup
1 tsp Dijon mustard

Slice the strawberries lengthways. You should get 4 or 5 slices from each strawberry.

Make the dressing by whisking together the oil, lemon juice, maple syrup and mustard in a small bowl, or shaking them in a jar.

In a large bowl, mix the rocket, spinach and basil and dress with 2 tablespoons of the dressing. Divide the strawberry slices and leaves between four plates then place a burrata on top of each arrangement. Drizzle a spoonful of dressing over each burrata, season with salt and 5 to 6 grinds of black pepper and serve.

Mango, Coriander and Couscous Salad

An easy way to get cubes of mango from a whole one is to cut the wide flat sides away from the stone with the skin still on. Then slice a grid into the flesh without cutting through the skin. Push the skin side of the mango piece so it turns inside out, and little skyscrapers of mango will pop up, ready for you to easily slice them off. Do this over the couscous so the juice goes in too. It's an old trick, but it's a goodie.

Serves 4

200g couscous

2 tbsp olive oil

zest and juice of 1 lime

1 large ripe mango, cut into 1cm cubes

½ cucumber, peeled, deseeded and cut into 1cm cubes

1 red serrano chilli, deseeded and finely chopped

10g picked mint leaves, finely chopped

10g picked coriander leaves, finely chopped

½ tsp sea salt

Put the couscous in a large heat-proof bowl and pour over 200ml of boiling water. Cover the bowl with cling film or a lid and leave to steam till soft, about 8 to 10 minutes. Remove the covering, fluff the couscous with a fork and add the olive oil. Add the lime zest and juice, mango, cucumber, chilli, mint, coriander and salt. Gently mix to bring everything together and serve.

Green Beans with Lemon and Mustard

This is a really delicious way to enjoy green beans. I've blanched them here for some sweet crunch, but you could easily toss them in oil and blister them in a hot pan. Try adding toasted walnuts or crumbled feta to this salad if you feel like changing things up a bit.

Serves 4

500g green beans, trimmed
salt

for the dressing:
1 tbsp wholegrain mustard
zest and juice of 1 lemon
2 tbsp extra virgin olive oil
1 tsp honey or maple syrup
1 garlic clove, grated
1 banana shallot, very thinly
  sliced
sea salt and freshly ground
  black pepper

Cook the beans in a large pan of salted simmering water for 3 to 4 minutes, then drain and refresh briefly under the cold water tap to stop them cooking. Drain well to ensure you don't add water to the dressing.

To make the dressing, add the mustard, lemon zest and juice, oil, honey or maple syrup, garlic and salt and pepper to a large bowl and whisk for about a minute, until emulsified. Then add the beans and the shallot to the bowl, mixing to ensure everything is evenly coated in the dressing, and serve.

88

Sesame Miso Noodle Salad

A cool way to garnish this salad is to make spring onion 'noodles'. Simply trim the spring onions and slice them neatly into long, thin strips 2–3cm wide. Leave in iced water for thirty minutes and they will curl into noodle-y springs.

Serves 4

250g egg noodles (4 nests)

4–5 spring onions, trimmed and finely chopped at an angle

1 tsp olive oil

2 tbsp sesame seeds

1 tsp red chilli flakes

100g cavolo nero, stems removed, finely chopped

200g sugar snap peas, finely sliced

10g picked mint leaves, chopped

salt

for the dressing:

2 tbsp extra virgin olive oil

2 tbsp miso paste

1 tbsp sesame oil

zest and juice of 1 lime

1 tbsp white wine vinegar

1 tbsp soy sauce

5cm piece of fresh ginger, grated

Cook the noodles in salted boiling water for 4 minutes, or according to the instructions on the packet. When tender, drain and rinse under cold water to halt cooking. While the noodles are cooking, prepare the dressing by whisking together the olive oil, miso, sesame oil, lime zest and juice, vinegar, soy sauce and ginger in a large bowl.

Fry the spring onions in a teaspoon of olive oil over a high heat until they start to brown, then turn off the heat and add the sesame seeds and chilli flakes.

Add the noodles to the large bowl with the dressing and toss gently, then add the cavolo nero, peas and mint. Mix gently to combine, then transfer to a serving bowl. Finally, garnish with a sprinkle of the spicy spring onions and serve.

Smashed Cucumber Salad

Smashing cucumbers isn't just gratuitously violent fun;
the light dressing clings to the newly bashed craggy
interior. This salad improves with an hour or so of resting
in the fridge, so it's cold and intense when you eat it
– ideally, with Sesame Miso Noodle Salad (see p.90).

Serves 4

2 cucumbers, ends trimmed
15g coriander, finely
   chopped
1 red serrano chilli, thinly
   sliced
2 tbsp sesame seeds

for the dressing:
2 tbsp rice wine vinegar
1 tbsp soy sauce
1 tbsp sesame oil
1 garlic clove, grated

Make the dressing in a wide shallow bowl by
whisking together the vinegar, soy sauce,
oil and garlic.

Wrap the cucumber loosely in cling film or a
clean tea towel and, using a rolling pin, bash it
four or five times along its length. Aim to crack
the cucumber and break it apart rather than pulp
it. Unwrap it and slice it into even pieces on a
diagonal. Add the cucumber to the bowl with the
dressing and sprinkle over the chopped coriander
and the chilli.

Toast the sesame seeds in a dry frying pan until
they start to turn golden and shiny (about 2 to 3
minutes) and add them to the cucumber. Leave
to marinate for a minimum of 15 minutes but
preferably an hour before serving.

There's a new, crisp freshness in the air. Harvest season is here. Grocers and farmers' markets are full of tomatoes, corn on the cob and cheeses made from milk made sweet by herby green pastures. You'll find plump, dark fruit like figs and brambles. Salads become more substantial now. Think wild rice and roasted beans, maybe the addition of smoky bacon to fortify tangy apples and Pecorino.

September

Ratatouille Salad

This is a true celebration of the end of summer and the beginning of autumn. I like to add a handful or three of Croutons (see p.137) to soak up the dressing.

Serves 4

1 medium aubergine, sliced into rounds
1 courgette, sliced on the bias
1 red pepper, deseeded and cut into wide strips
1 red onion, cut into eighths
3 tbsp extra virgin olive oil
50g pine nuts, toasted
400g sweet cherry tomatoes
4 cloves garlic, sliced thinly
5g picked thyme leaves
5g picked rosemary leaves
25g picked basil leaves
1 tsp chilli flakes (optional)
1 quantity Balsamic Reduction (p.137)
sea salt and freshly ground black pepper

Preheat the oven to 210°C/190°C fan. Put the aubergine, courgette, red pepper and onion into a large roasting tray and toss in the olive oil and a teaspoon of salt. Slide the tray onto the top shelf of the oven and set a timer for 35 minutes.

Meanwhile, toast the pine nuts in a dry frying pan for 2 or 3 minutes, or until golden.

When the timer goes off, add the tomatoes, garlic, thyme and rosemary to the tray and, using a spatula, turn so that everything is incorporated. Continue to roast for another 10 minutes, or until everything is golden and fragrant and the tomatoes have started to pop and frizzle.

Remove from the oven and transfer everything to a serving dish then scatter over the pine nuts, basil and chilli flakes, if using. Finally, check the seasoning and adjust to your liking, and add a dramatic squiggle of balsamic reduction.

Za'atar Sweet Potatoes with Figs

I often throw a couple of mild red chillies in to roast with the sweet potatoes. They will char nicely, and you can just chop and scatter them over the finished salad.

Serves 4

2 tbsp za'atar
3 tbsp extra virgin olive oil
3 medium sweet potatoes, scrubbed
1 × 400g tin of butter or borlotti beans, drained and rinsed
6 garlic cloves, unpeeled
180g rocket
5g picked thyme and rosemary leaves, finely chopped
4 ripe figs, quartered
salt and freshly ground black pepper

for the dressing:
1 tbsp balsamic vinegar
1 tbsp extra virgin olive oil
1 tsp Dijon mustard

Preheat the oven to 200°C/180°C fan. In a large bowl, whisk the za'atar into the olive oil. Cut the sweet potatoes into even 2cm cubes and mix into the spiced oil along with the beans, garlic and half a teaspoon of salt. Then tip everything onto a roasting tray in a single layer and roast for 30 minutes, until the sweet potato is tender and caramelised and the beans are tender on the bottom and pleasingly crisp on top.

Make the dressing by whisking together the balsamic vinegar, olive oil and mustard.

Toss the rocket in the dressing and fold gently through the warm sweet potato and beans in a serving dish. Then scatter over the thyme and rosemary and arrange the quartered figs on top. Finally, season generously and serve.

September

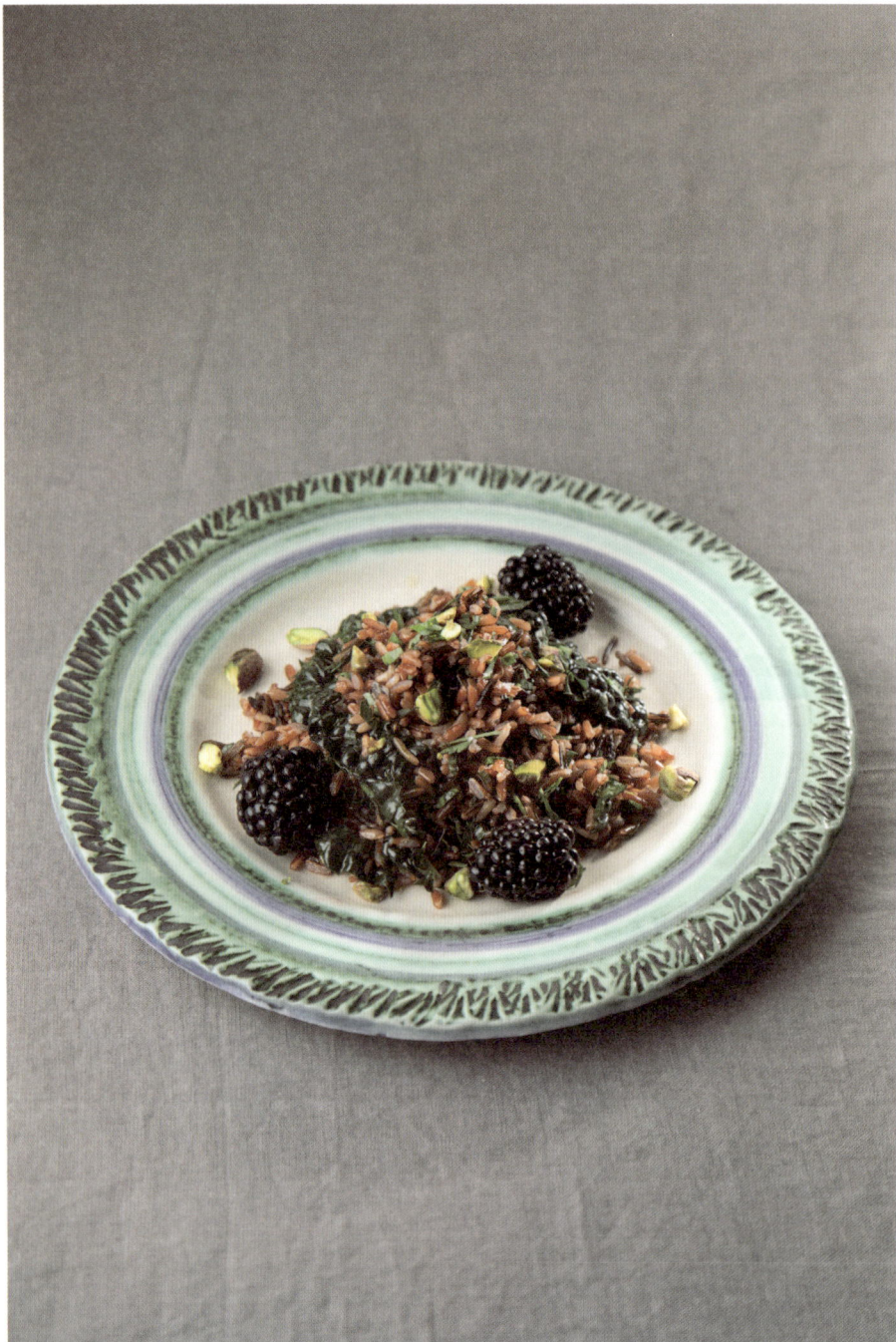

Wild Rice, Bramble and Pistachio Salad

The dark brambles add a sweet sharpness to the earthy rice and give a definite sparkle to this salad. I add red currants too if I can find them. Blueberries or blackcurrants would work just as well if you've missed bramble picking. You'll find red Camargue rice mixed with wild rice in most large supermarkets, but any wild rice mix could be substituted here.

Serves 4

170g red Camargue and wild rice or other wild rice mix (approx. 350g cooked rice)
200g kale (Russian kale, cavolo nero, curly kale or a mix)
50g shelled pistachios
10g picked tarragon leaves, finely chopped
10g picked flat-leaf parsley leaves, finely chopped
200g brambles
sea salt and freshly ground black pepper

for the dressing:
1 tablespoon red wine vinegar
1 tsp wholegrain mustard
¼ tsp sugar
2 tbsp extra virgin olive oil

Cook the rice according to the packet instructions. Remove the big stems from the kale and tear it into pieces. Then chop or bash the pistachios until you can see their emerald interiors.

Make the dressing by whisking together the vinegar, mustard, sugar and oil.

While the rice is still warm (not hot), add the dressing and the kale – so the kale tenderises in the warm dressing – and stir through the tarragon and parsley. Transfer the salad to a serving dish and scatter over the brambles and pistachios, then season and serve.

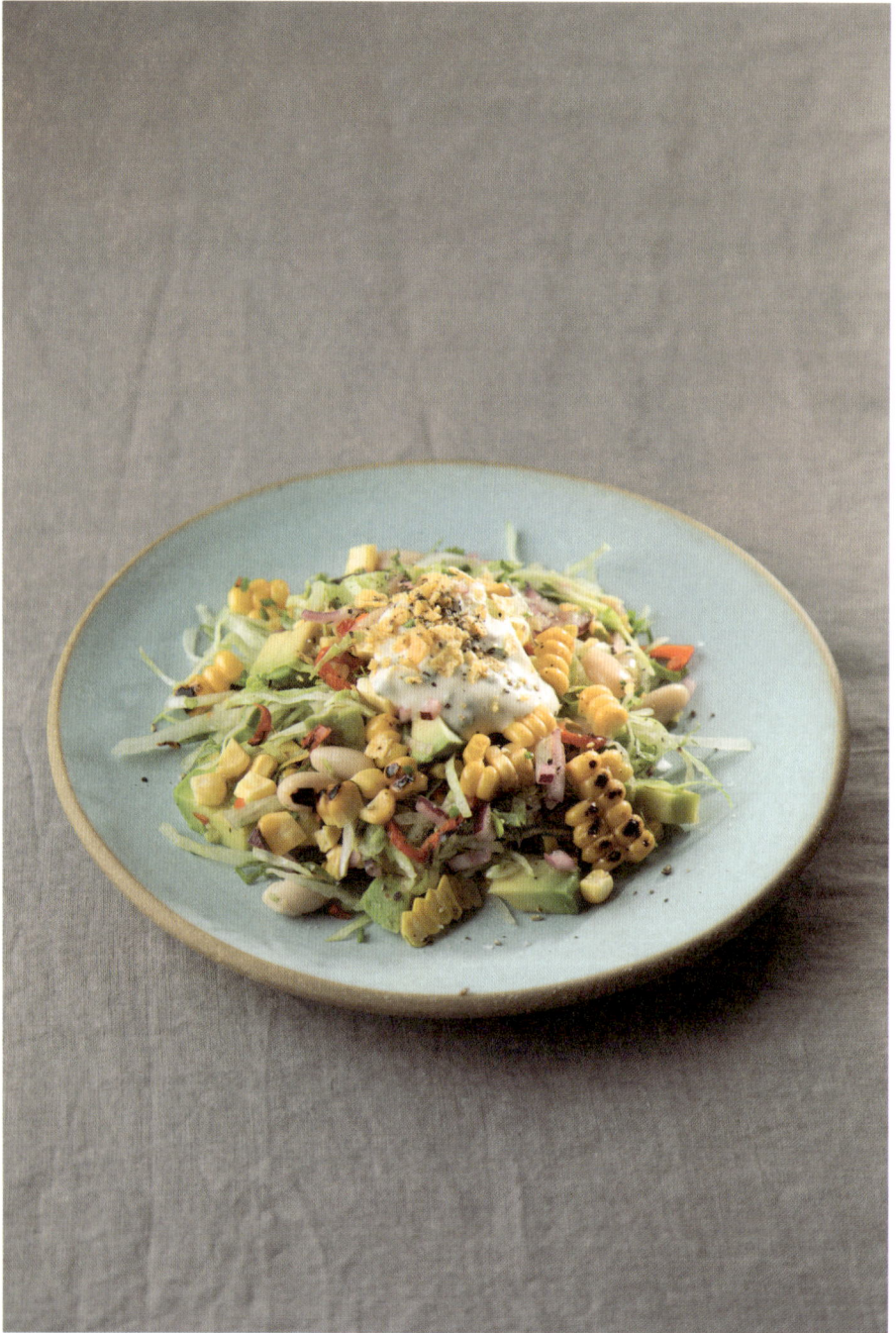

Chargrilled Corn Salad with Ranch Dressing

Some salads are made for quick lunches, some are for celebrations. This one falls into the latter category. It's a party favourite as the different elements can be prepared in advance. Then you simply dress it and sprinkle over the tortillas at the last minute.

Serves 4

2 cobs of corn
1 tbsp extra virgin olive oil
2 mild red chillies
zest and juice of 1 lemon
1 red onion, finely diced
1 ripe avocado, diced
2 × 400g tins cannellini beans
1 medium iceberg lettuce, finely chopped
25g coriander, roughly chopped
100g tortilla chips, finely crumbled
sea salt and freshly ground black pepper

for the ranch dressing:
350g mayonnaise or vegenaise
2 tbsp white wine vinegar
1 clove garlic, grated
1 tsp onion powder
10g chives, finely chopped

Brush the corn cobs with the oil, then season them. Heat a ribbed grill pan or frying pan over high heat. Sear the corn and the whole chillies, turning them often using tongs, so they are cooked all the way 'round and charred in places. Remove from the heat and set aside to cool.

To make the dressing, whisk the mayo, vinegar, garlic, onion powder and chives together in a bowl.

Mix the lemon zest and juice with the red onion and avocado in a bowl and leave to marinate. Deseed and chop the roasted chillies and put them in a bowl along with the beans, lettuce and coriander. Once the corn has cooled, cut the kernels from the cob (by standing it upright on a board and slicing down using a serrated knife, a bit like carving meat from a doner kebab).

Add the corn and the red onion and avocado (along with the lemon juice) to the salad and mix to combine, then spoon over the dressing, season and scatter over the tortilla chips as a final flourish.

Misty mornings and shortening days mean it is time to be cosy. It's a time to enjoy the colours of the changing trees, clementines and beetroot. Pyramids of pumpkins come to mind as do spices like cinnamon and paprika that warm from the inside.

October

Spiced Beetroot and Clementine Salad

This is mulled wine-marinated beetroot – the cinnamon and brown sugar soften it and enhance its earthiness. You could turn this salad into a more substantial lunch by adding cooked whole grains such as farro or pearl barley and two or three handfuls of baby spinach.

Serves 4

300g cooked beetroot
3 thin-skinned clementines
120ml red wine
160ml sherry vinegar
2–3 bay leaves
80g brown sugar
2 star anise
1 cinnamon stick
50g shelled pistachios

Slice the beetroot into circles about the thickness of a pound coin. Peel the clementines, reserving the skins, and slice into very thin circles too – you will need to be nimble fingered.

In a medium pan, bring the wine, vinegar, bay leaves, sugar, star anise, cinnamon stick and 120ml water to a simmer, and stir gently till the sugar has dissolved. Add the beetroot slices then remove from the heat and set aside to cool in the tangy sweet and sour sauce. Drain when cool.

Take a couple of pieces of peel (about 5g) and cut the white pith from the back, so you're left with just the bright orange peel. Now finely chop it with the pistachios so you have a beautiful green and orange chopped rubble (rather than a dust).

Arrange the beetroot and clementine slices on a serving plate, scatter over the pistachio clementine rubble and serve.

Sesame Miso Aubergine Salad

Shichimi togarashi is a spicy blend of chilli, seeds, spices and citrus peel – it's worth seeking out. The deal with the chickpeas here is that some stay in the aubergine and some tumble onto the tray to roast and become crispy, like bonus croutons.

Serves 4

2 large aubergines, halved lengthways
90ml olive oil
2 garlic cloves, crushed
1 tbsp brown sugar
1 tbsp white miso
2 tbsp tamari
2 tbsp sesame seeds
1 × 400g tin chickpeas, drained, rinsed and patted dry
1 tbsp balsamic vinegar
1 tsp shichimi togarashi or chilli powder
100g pomegranate seeds
25g coriander, roughly chopped
25g pea shoots

Preheat the oven to 190°C/170°C fan. Score the cut flesh-sides of the aubergine halves in a diamond cross-hatch pattern. Place the aubergines on a baking tray, cut sides up.

In a medium bowl, whisk together the oil, garlic, sugar, miso, tamari and sesame seeds. Brush about 2 tablespoons of this mixture over the flesh and roast in the oven for 15 minutes.

Remove the aubergines from the oven and add the chickpeas, piling a handful on each half and pushing them into the softening flesh. Any that fall off will crisp up as they roast. Brush another 2 or 3 tablespoons of the mixture over the chickpeas and aubergines then bake for another 30 minutes, or until the aubergines are brown and tender. Remove from the oven and allow to cool. Whisk the vinegar into the remaining mixture to make a dressing. Transfer the aubergines to a serving plate. Sprinkle the togarashi over the crispy chickpeas left in the baking tray and scatter these over the aubergines. Then top with the pomegranate seeds and scatter over the coriander and pea shoots. Finally, drizzle over the finished dressing and serve.

October

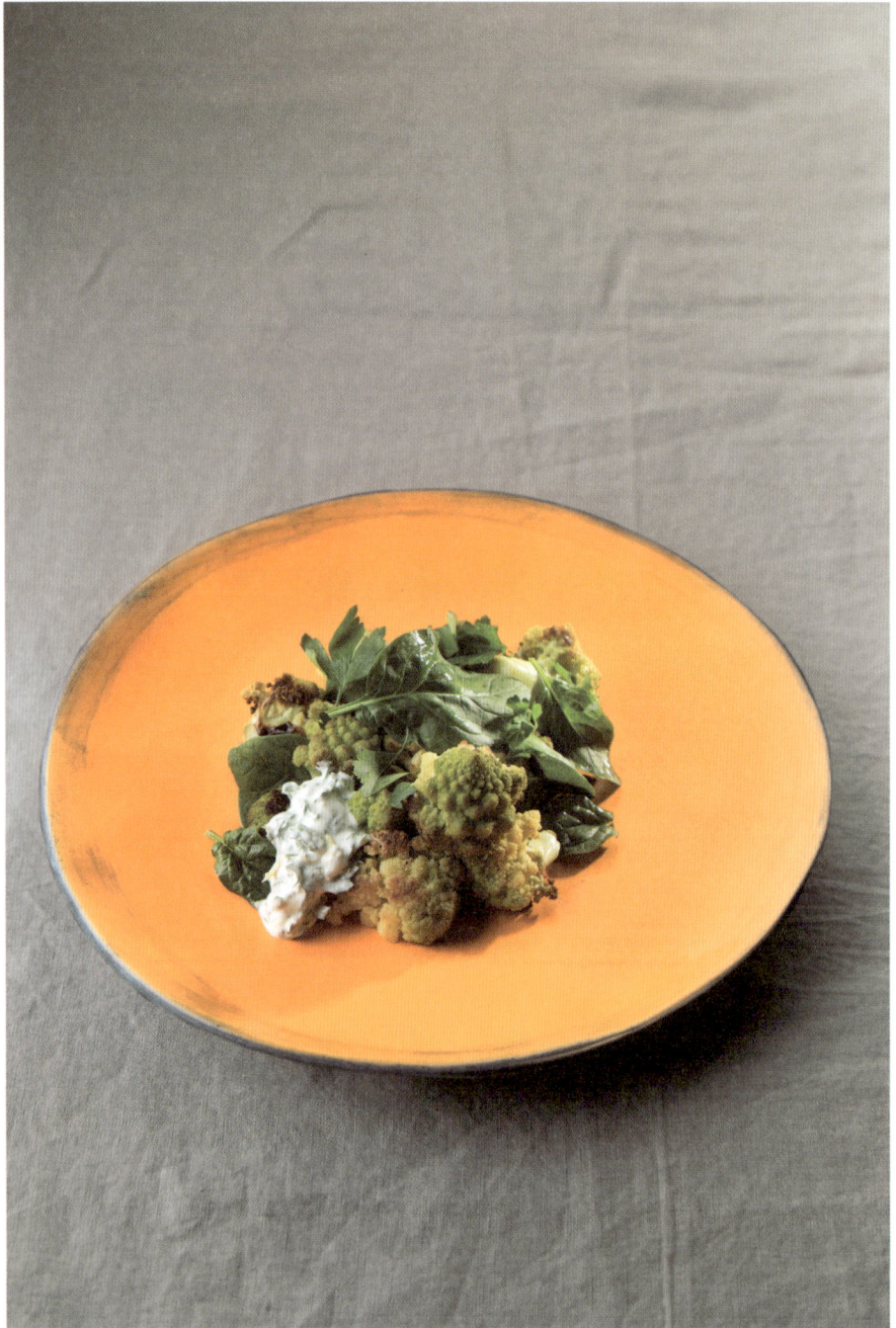

Romanesco with Herb Crème Fraîche

A beautifully exotic-looking lime green fractal, romanesco is a cousin of the cauliflower but slightly sweeter and less peppery. Choose a tight dense head when selecting. Its crisp leaves could also be chopped and added to this salad. Dukkah (see p.138) would be delicious sprinkled over the crème fraîche here.

Serves 4

1 medium romanesco, trimmed
2 tbsp extra virgin olive oil
1 tsp sea salt
25g butter
200g baby spinach

for the herb crème fraîche:
10g picked oregano leaves, very finely chopped
finely grated zest of 1 lemon
1 garlic clove, grated
30g picked flat-leaf parsley leaves, finely chopped (reserve half to garnish)
300ml crème fraîche, Greek yoghurt or vegan alternative

Preheat the oven to 200°C/180°C fan. Pull the romanesco into florets and chop the stalk. Transfer to a large roasting dish and toss in the oil and salt then dot over the butter. Roast for 15 to 20 minutes, shaking the tray after 10 minutes to ensure even distribution of the butter.

Meanwhile, make the herb crème fraîche by mixing the oregano, lemon zest, garlic and half the chopped parsley into the crème fraîche or yoghurt.

When the romanesco is tender and slightly browned, remove it from the oven and allow it to cool slightly, then add the spinach and mix gently so everything is well coated in the residual oil. Transfer to a serving dish, sprinkle with the reserved parsley and serve with a generous spoonful of the herb crème fraîche.

Apple, Caramelised Walnuts and Pecorino

This is everything I look for in a salad. The balance between the bittersweet walnuts, sharp apple and salty cheese is simple and perfect.

Serves 4

120g walnuts
2 tbsp maple syrup
pinch of sea salt
2 apples, cored and thinly sliced
2 sticks celery, thinly sliced
300g juicy leaves such as baby spinach, rocket or nasturtium or a mix
100g Pecorino

for the dressing:
2 tbsp smooth apple sauce
1 tbsp cider vinegar
2 tbsp extra virgin olive oil
1 tsp wholegrain mustard
¼ tsp sea salt

First make the dressing by whisking together the apple sauce, vinegar, oil, mustard and salt in a bowl then set it aside.

Toast the walnuts in a dry, non-stick frying pan over a medium heat until they begin to darken and become fragrant, about 2 to 3 minutes. With a wooden spatula at the ready, add the maple syrup to the pan and mix until all the walnuts are covered. This should take 15 to 20 seconds. Then tip everything out in a single layer onto greaseproof paper, sprinkle with a pinch of sea salt and leave to set.

Arrange the apple and celery over the leaves in a serving dish and dress the salad a tablespoon at a time until it's dressed to your liking. Then top with the candied walnuts and, using a kitchen knife or vegetable peeler, shave thin curls of Pecorino over the salad and serve.

Spicy Roasted Pumpkin with Brown Rice and Pumpkin Seeds

Use this recipe to explore the world of esoteric pumpkins. I find their beautiful shapes and colours irresistible. Varieties like kabocha and Blue Hokkaido are delicious here but so are acorn and butternut squash and you can toast the seeds in just the same way. If I'm making this for a party, I'll add 50g toasted pine nuts.

Serves 4

250g brown rice (approx. 450g cooked brown rice)
½ medium-sized kabocha pumpkin with seeds (approx. 700g)
2 tbsp extra virgin olive oil
5cm piece of fresh ginger, grated
1 tsp ground cinnamon
1 tsp maple syrup
1 tsp chilli flakes (plus a little more for sprinkling)
200g rocket
juice and zest of 1 lemon
sea salt

Preheat the oven to 180°C/160°C fan. Simmer the rice in 500ml water with 1 teaspoon of salt added for 40 minutes, or according to the packet instructions.

Cut the pumpkin in half across the circumference, scrape the seeds out (reserving them), and cut the pumpkin into crescent moon shapes. Rinse the seeds and pat dry. Put the pumpkin and seeds, oil, ginger, cinnamon, maple syrup, chilli flakes and half a teaspoon of salt in a large bowl and mix until everything is well coated in the spicy oil.

Tip everything onto a large baking tray or a roasting tin lined with greaseproof paper and roast for 25 minutes, or until the pumpkin is tender and golden. Remove from the oven and, when cool enough to handle, peel off the skin and add the pumpkin and the seeds to the rice in a large bowl. Then add the rocket, lemon zest and juice and mix gently to combine. Finally, check for salt and add another sprinkle of chilli flakes if you're in the mood.

October

We are on the cusp of winter with darker afternoons and often stormy skies. It's a time to enjoy soft roasted vegetables and spicy dressed grains, to appreciate fragrant additions such as sharp, tangy apple slices and rosemary with its resinous scent. Here are salads to comfort and strengthen.

November

Pearl Couscous with Miso Lemon Mushrooms

If you can get hold of golden chanterelles or girolles when they're in season, they would work perfectly in this recipe. In general, you can forage or buy these wild mushrooms in Scotland between June and November. Preserved lemon is a delicious addition here. They're readily available but it's very easy to preserve your own (see p.139).

Serves 4

2 tbsp extra virgin olive oil

4 portobello mushrooms, thinly sliced

8 chestnut mushrooms, thinly sliced

350g pearl couscous

1 tbsp preserved lemon, finely chopped

zest of ½ lemon

10g each of picked parsley, chervil and mint leaves, roughly chopped

100g Pecorino

sea salt and freshly ground black pepper

for the dressing:

25g butter

1 tsp miso paste mixed with 2 tsp water

juice of ½ lemon

5g picked lemon thyme leaves

In a heavy-based frying pan, heat the oil and fry the portobello and chestnut mushrooms until they're golden. Season well.

Transfer the mushrooms to a plate, then make the dressing by adding the butter and miso to the hot pan. Let it melt and come to a simmer, then stir in the lemon juice and thyme and remove from the heat.

Bring a large pot of salted water to the boil, add the couscous, bring back to a simmer and cook until tender, about 8 to 10 minutes, or according to the packet instructions. Drain and leave to cool in a sieve over the pan.

Mix the dressing, mushrooms, preserved lemon, lemon zest and parsley, chervil and mint into the warm couscous and check for seasoning. Finally, divide between plates and grate or, preferably, shave curls of, Pecorino over the top.

118

Sweet Orange and Date Freekeh with Roast Parsnips

Freekeh is a firm, chewy wheat grain that has a roasted smoky flavour because it's picked green and then has the green husks burnt off. It's highly nutritious and really delicious.

Serves 4

500g parsnips, peeled
2 red onions, peeled
2 garlic cloves, skin left on
3 tbsp extra virgin olive oil
1 tsp ground cinnamon
1 tsp ground allspice
½ tsp salt
2 tbsp maple syrup
200g freekeh
1 bay leaf
100g dates, stoned and chopped
50g cranberries
10g chives, finely chopped
sea salt and freshly ground black pepper

for the dressing:
3 tbsp extra virgin olive oil
1 tbsp sherry vinegar
zest and juice of 1 small orange

Preheat your oven to 200°C/180°C fan. Quarter the parsnips lengthways and cut out any woody cores. Halve the onions lengthways and cut them into chunky crescents. Put the parsnips, onion and garlic into a roasting dish and toss well in the oil, cinnamon, allspice, salt and maple syrup. Cover with foil and roast for 20 minutes, then take the foil off, give everything a shake and roast uncovered for another 15 minutes, or until the parsnips are tender and the onions have started to caramelise.

Meanwhile roast the freekeh with the bay leaf in a dry pan for 2 or 3 minutes, then add 400ml water and a teaspoon of salt. Bring to a boil, then turn down the heat and simmer for 20 minutes. When the freekeh is tender, drain it and cool it on a baking tray. Scatter over the dates and cranberries so they plump up. Make the dressing by whisking together the oil, vinegar and orange zest and juice. Peel the roast garlic, mash it with a fork and add it to the dressing. Then stir the dressing a spoonful at a time into the freekeh, taking care not to overdress. Season to taste then transfer to a serving platter, arrange the parsnips and onions on top and scatter over the chives.

120

Butternut Squash, Gnocchi and Rocket with Spiced Orange Dressing

It's slightly unusual to roast gnocchi, but cooking it this way is so easy and makes it wonderfully chewy and crispy, perfect for a spicy, warm winter salad.

Serves 4

½ medium butternut squash, peeled and deseeded (approx. 600g)
500g good-quality gnocchi
3–5 tbsp olive oil
¼ tsp cayenne pepper
¼ tsp ground allspice
½ tsp ground cinnamon
1 tsp maple syrup
100g hazelnuts, roughly chopped
200g rocket
sea salt and freshly ground black pepper

for the dressing:
oil from the roasting tin
zest and juice of 1 orange

Preheat the oven to 180°C/160°C fan. Cut the squash into gnocchi-sized cubes and place in a shallow-sided roasting tray along with the gnocchi, oil, cayenne pepper, allspice, cinnamon, maple syrup, hazelnuts and a quarter teaspoon of sea salt. Mix well so everything is coated in the oil and spices, and roast in the oven for 25 to 30 minutes, giving the tray a shake halfway through cooking. Add a little more oil if it's starting to dry out. When done, the butternut squash will be tender and the gnocchi will have crisped and puffed up. Lift everything out of the pan and transfer to a large serving bowl, carefully reserving the oil in the tray. To make the dressing, add the orange zest and juice to the tray and whisk it into the oil, scraping up the spices and crispy bits.

Sprinkle the rocket over the warm ingredients in the bowl, drizzle over the dressing, and toss gently one or two times until everything has just come together. Check for seasoning and serve.

Fennel, Apple and Cabbage Slaw

Savoy cabbage isn't usually used in a slaw, but in the dark winter months I crave the chlorophyl hit of the green. It becomes tender when marinated in the tangy dressing here.

Serves 4

500g savoy or sweetheart
  (hispi) cabbage
1 head of fennel with fronds
  reserved for garnish
1 red onion, peeled
1 apple

for the dressing:
juice and zest of 1 lime
30ml cider vinegar
50ml extra virgin olive oil
1 tsp caraway seeds
pinch of sea salt

Chop the cabbage and fennel into shreds and finely chop the red onion. Core and finely slice the apple.

Make the dressing by whisking the lime juice and zest, vinegar, oil, caraway seeds and salt together in a large bowl. Add the sliced ingredients and mix well. Garnish with the fennel fronds and serve.

December

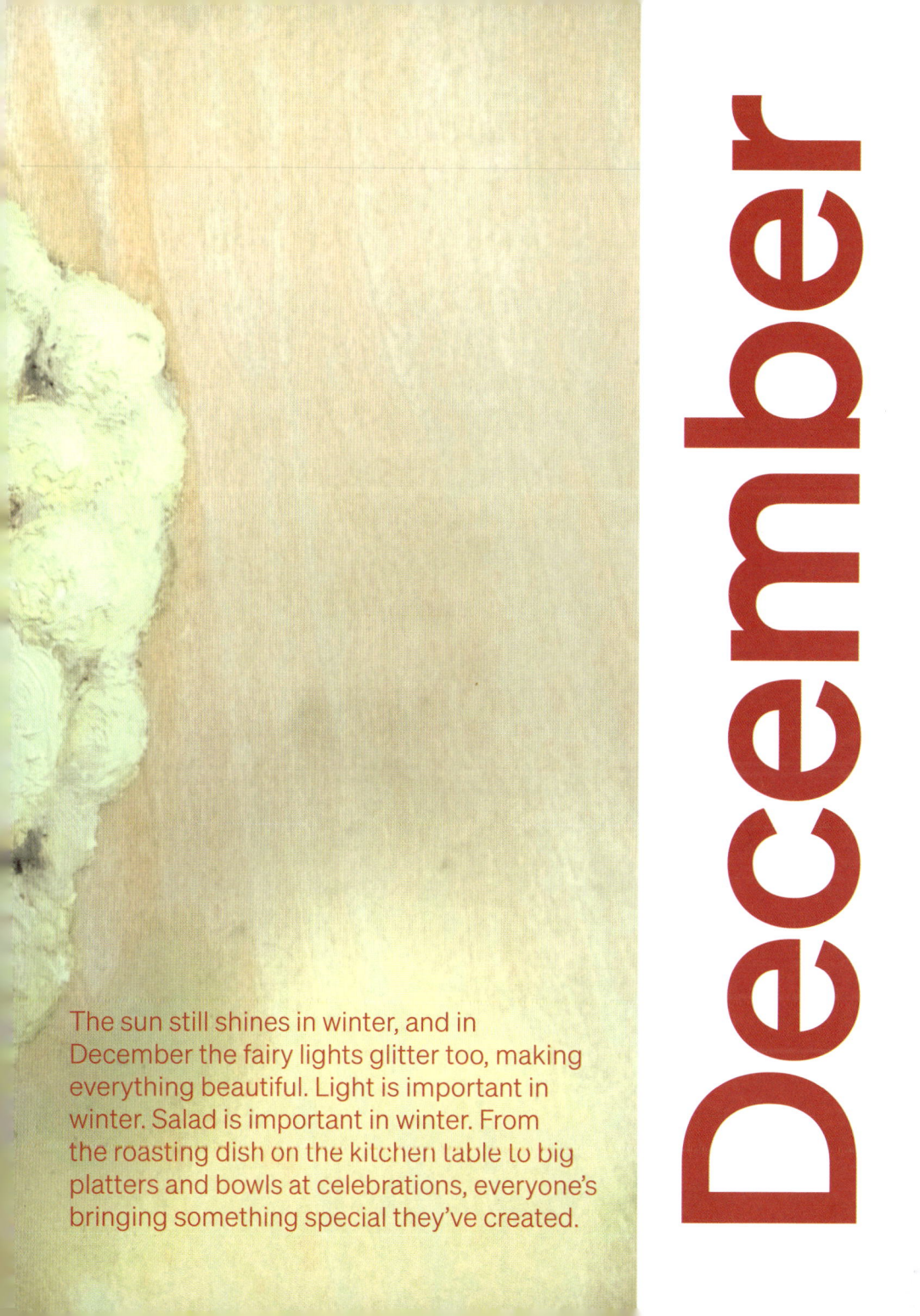

The sun still shines in winter, and in December the fairy lights glitter too, making everything beautiful. Light is important in winter. Salad is important in winter. From the roasting dish on the kitchen table to big platters and bowls at celebrations, everyone's bringing something special they've created.

Jerusalem Artichoke, Apple and Chestnut Salad

I have chosen endive here because of its white lightning strike pattern and intense colour, but I love its insistent bitterness too. It offsets the sweet earthiness of the chestnuts and artichokes. Chestnuts are an underappreciated hero in winter salads; they're so sweet when they're cooked – irresistible!

Serves 4

2 tbsp extra virgin olive oil

400g Jerusalem artichokes, scrubbed (and peeled, if preferred)

180g chestnuts, cooked and peeled

200–300g endive or other bitter leaf (p.140), torn

1 large Cox's Orange Pippin, cored and thinly sliced

sea salt and freshly ground black pepper

for the dressing:

1 banana shallot, finely chopped

1 tbsp wholegrain mustard

2 tbsp sherry vinegar

1 tbsp maple syrup

4 tbsp extra virgin olive oil

¼ tsp sea salt

Preheat the oven to 180°C/160°C fan. Pour the oil into a roasting pan and season it well with salt and pepper. Cut the artichokes into chestnut-sized pieces and add them to the roasting pan, giving everything a good shake to coat it in oil. Roast for 35 minutes, then add the chestnuts and roast for another 5 minutes. When ready, the artichokes will be tender on the inside and crispy on the outside. Remove the pan from the oven and set aside.

Make the dressing by whisking together the shallot, mustard, vinegar, maple syrup, oil and salt. Arrange the endive on a serving dish and scatter over the apple slices followed by the warm chestnuts and artichokes. Dress the salad a tablespoon at a time, tasting until it's to your satisfaction, then season and serve.

December

Spiced Cauliflower with Herb Oil

Don't forget to include the stem of the cauliflower here so nothing is wasted – it's all delicious. Roasting the cauliflower really brings out its wonderful flavour. You can crush the whole coriander seeds in a mortar and pestle if you prefer – my tastes are rustic so I don't bother.

Serves 4

1 smallish head of cauliflower

50ml olive oil

1 tbsp coriander seeds, crushed if preferred

1 tsp fennel seeds

1 tsp turmeric

1 tsp chilli flakes

3 garlic cloves, finely chopped

½ tsp sea salt

1 quantity Herb Oil (p.136)

300ml Greek yoghurt to serve (optional)

Preheat the oven to 210°C/190°C fan. Break the cauliflower into small florets and chop the leftover stem into similar-sized pieces.

In a large bowl whisk the olive oil together with the coriander and fennel seeds, turmeric, chilli flakes, garlic and salt. Add the cauliflower and mix well then transfer to a roasting tin and roast on the top shelf of the oven for 25 to 30 minutes, or until the cauliflower is tender, fragrant and well caramelised at the edges.

When the cauliflower is ready, arrange it on a serving plate, spoon over the herb oil and serve warm. I sometimes serve this with a cool dollop of Greek yoghurt on the side.

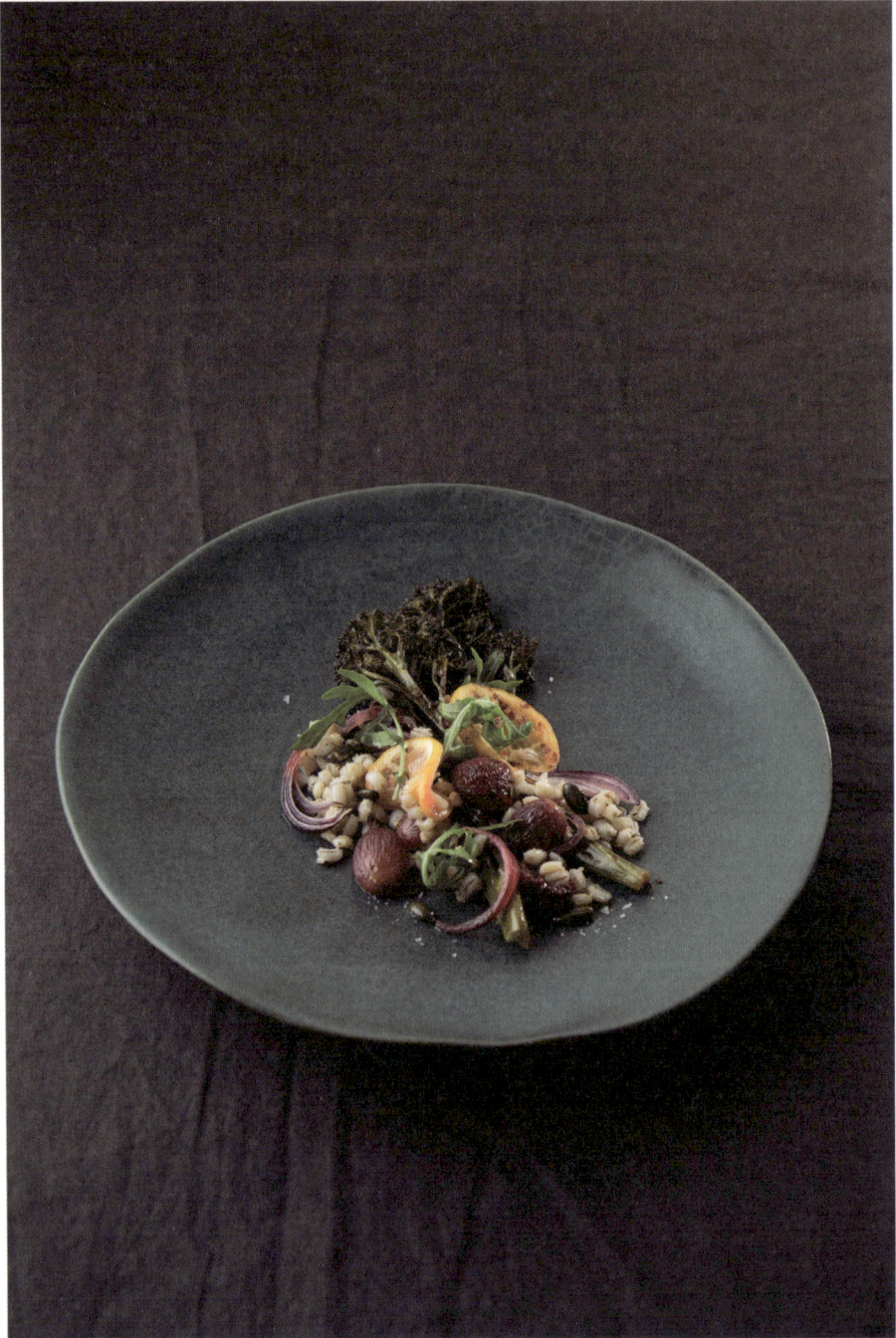

Barley with Purple Sprouting Broccoli

A big kitchen time-hack for me is having precooked wholegrains handy in the fridge or freezer. I always make a big batch as it takes just as much effort to cook a large quantity as it does a small one. A ready supply is very handy for our household, who are 'never not hungry'. I often serve this right out of the roasting tin.

Serves 4

200g barley (approx. 500g cooked barley)
1 lemon
3 tbsp extra virgin olive oil
300g purple sprouting broccoli, washed and trimmed
1 red onion, finely sliced
200g red seedless grapes
30g pumpkin seeds
½ tsp red chilli flakes
2 rosemary sprigs, picked and finely chopped
30g rocket
sea salt and freshly ground black pepper

Preheat the oven to 210°C/190°C fan. Cover the barley with plenty of cold water in a large pan, bring to the boil and simmer for about 30 minutes, until tender, then drain well.

Halve the lemon and cut one half into thin slices. Drizzle the oil over the base of a baking dish and add the broccoli, onion, grapes, lemon slices and pumpkin seeds. Mix so everything is coated in oil, then season with the chilli flakes and a decent pinch of salt.

Roast for 20 minutes, until the broccoli tips are charred and the grapes are roasted plump-to-bursting. Once out of the oven, scatter over the cooked barley and rosemary, give it a stir to incorporate the hot oil and squeeze over the juice from the leftover lemon half. Check for seasoning, scatter over the rocket and serve.

Pear, Walnut and Sautéed Date Salad

Dates seared in hot oil and finished with a pinch of sea salt are one of the best Christmas treats you could give yourself. This is a simple, happy dish – perfect for parties.

Serves 4

3 tbsp extra virgin olive oil
12 Medjool dates, pitted
juice of 1 lemon
1 tsp maple syrup or honey
200g rocket
2–3 ripe Bartlett or Bosc pears, cored and sliced lengthways
50g walnuts
sea salt

Heat the oil in a frying pan over a medium heat and sauté the dates, allowing 1 or 2 minutes on each side. Transfer the dates to a plate and sprinkle with a pinch of sea salt.

Pour the warm oil from the dates into a bowl and whisk in the lemon juice and the maple syrup or honey.

Scatter the rocket on a serving plate and arrange the pear slices and walnuts on top, then drizzle over the dressing, scatter over the warm dates and serve.

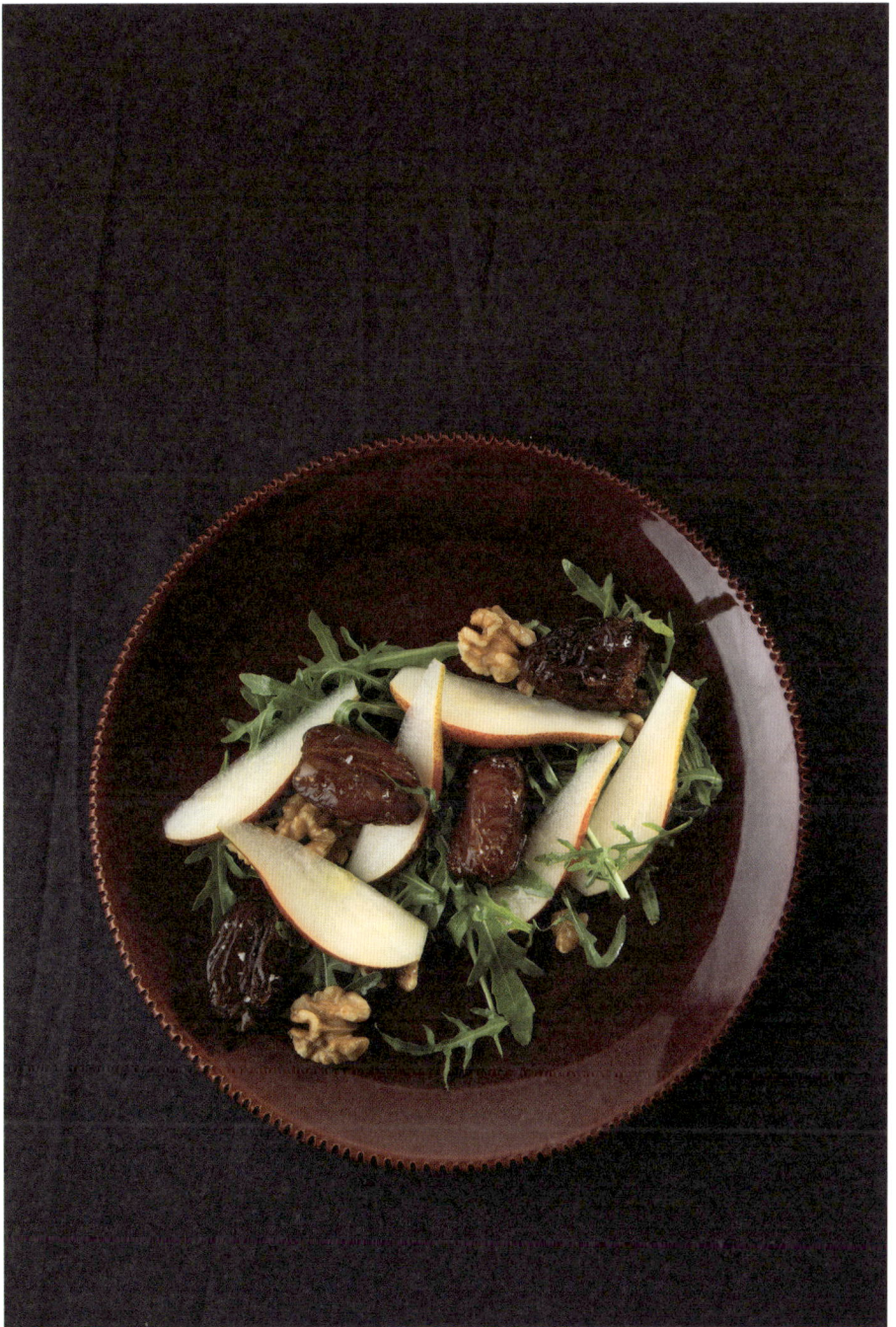

Delicious Additions

Here are some simple recipes for adding flavour, texture and substance to a salad. Many of these additions are commonly shop bought but are easier than you'd expect to prepare at home – and often taste much better as a result. You also have the advantage of being able to customise to your own liking.

Mayonnaise

2 egg yolks
¼ tsp salt
2 tbsp lemon juice
450ml sunflower oil

Whisk the egg yolks, salt and lemon juice until they are well combined. Then slowly add the oil in a very thin stream, whisking all the time. Pause the oil every so often while you whisk to make sure it is properly incorporated. For never-fail mayo, use a handheld electric whisk – old school is the best school. If it should inexplicably split, slowly whisk in 1 teaspoon Dijon mustard to restore it to a smooth consistency.

Dijonnaise: add 1 tablespoon wholegrain Dijon mustard to the yolks and proceed as above.

Misonnaise: omit the salt and add 1 tablespoon miso paste to the yolks, then proceed as left and fold in 1 teaspoon lemon zest once everything has come together.

Aioli: add 1 teaspoon Dijon mustard and a grated garlic clove to the yolks then proceed as left.

Lemonnaise: make Mayonnaise as left, then stir in the zest and juice of half a lemon.

Baconnaise: make Mayonnaise as left, then add 1 teaspoon onion powder, 2 finely chopped rashers of very crispy, cooked, smoked streaky bacon and 1 tablespoon very finely chopped parsley.

Herb Oil

10g picked mint leaves
10g picked basil leaves
1 garlic clove
½ tsp sea salt
80ml extra virgin olive oil

Use a stick blender and blitz the mint, basil, garlic and salt until puréed, then add the oil and mix to combine. Alternatively, finely chop everything (except the oil) together or mash in a mortar and pestle then stir into the oil.

Balsamic Reduction

200ml balsamic vinegar

In a small pan over a medium heat, bring the balsamic to a boil then lower to a simmer for 5 to 7 minutes, until the vinegar has reduced by about half and is thick enough to coat the back of a spoon. It will thicken more as it cools. Transfer to a jar while warm if making in advance.

Croutons

2 slices of de-crusted bread (stale is fine)
1 garlic clove, cut in half lengthways
3 tbsp extra virgin olive oil
½ tsp fine sea salt

Preheat the oven to 200°C/180°C fan. Rub the bread on each side with the cut half of the garlic and cut or tear into 2–3cm cubes. Add the olive oil and salt to a large bowl and throw in the bread, mixing (ideally with your hands) to ensure it is well coated. Put the cubes on a baking tray and bake for 10 to 15 minutes, giving them a shake at the halfway mark. They are done when crisp and golden brown.

Spicy: add 1 teaspoon chilli powder.

Smoky: add 1 teaspoon smoked paprika.

Fragrant: add chopped rosemary and lemon zest.

Garlicky Breadcrumbs

2 tbsp extra virgin olive oil or 25g butter
1 garlic clove, grated
120g Panko breadcrumbs
¼ tsp sea salt

Optional additions: lemon zest, dried chilli flakes, chopped herbs such as thyme or chives, anchovies.

Heat the oil or butter in a frying pan, add the garlic, breadcrumbs, salt and any optional additions and cook gently for 8 to 10 minutes, until the crumbs absorb the oil and become brown and toasty.

Parmesan Shards

100g Parmesan, freshly grated
½ tsp cayenne pepper (optional)

Preheat the oven to 200°C/180°C fan. Line a baking sheet with greaseproof paper and sprinkle over the Parmesan. Bake for 8 to 10 minutes until the cheese is golden and bubbling. Once cool, sprinkle with the cayenne, if using, then break the cheese into shards. The shards will keep in an airtight container for 4 to 5 days.

Spiced Nuts

150g blanched almonds

150g pecans

150g cashews

30g pumpkin seeds

75g maple syrup

30ml extra olive oil

1 tablespoon rosemary
    leaves, finely chopped

2 tsp chilli flakes

1 tsp smoked paprika

1 tsp sea salt

Preheat the oven to
170°C /160°C fan. Combine
all the ingredients in a large
bowl, tip onto a baking
tray lined with greaseproof
paper and bake for 15
minutes. Set aside to cool
before eating. They will
keep in an airtight container
for at least 2 weeks.

Dukkah

1 tbsp cumin seeds

1 tbsp coriander seeds

1 tbsp fennel seeds

1 tbsp sesame seeds

50g hazelnuts

50g shelled pistachios or
    pine nuts

1 tsp dried oregano

½ tsp sea salt

Toast the cumin, coriander,
fennel and sesame seeds
over a medium heat in a
dry frying pan for 1 to 2
minutes, until they become
fragrant. Add these to the
remaining ingredients in a
food processor and pulse
until everything is chopped
into small pieces – but not
to dust. Dukkah will uplift
anything you add it to, be
it hummus or a boiled egg,
and will keep in a jar for at
least a couple of weeks.

Roasted Peppers

4 red, yellow or orange
    peppers, or a mix

2 or more garlic cloves,
    crushed (optional)

a sprig of rosemary
    (optional)

extra virgin olive oil to cover

Halve the peppers vertically
and remove the seeds,
then grill them under a hot
grill for about 10 minutes,
until the skins are blistered
and blackened. While still
hot, put them in a bowl
and cover (with a pan lid or
cling film), so they continue
to steam as they cool.
This should take about 10
minutes. The skins should
then easily rub off – I use
the blunt side of a knife to
scrape until they're clean.
Don't be tempted to wash
the skin off the peppers
as this can make them
flavourless and mushy. Then
transfer them to a jar with
the garlic and rosemary, if
using, and cover with the oil.
They'll keep very nicely like
this for at least a week.

Crispy Shallots

300ml sunflower oil

2 medium banana shallots,
    peeled and thinly sliced
    into rings

sea salt

In a medium saucepan,
heat the sunflower oil over
a moderate heat – it should
be at least 3cm deep in the
pan. Use one ring as a tester
and wait until it bubbles
when it hits the oil before
you add all the shallots.
Simmer them in the oil for
15 minutes, until they are
golden and crisp - keep
an eye on them though, as
once they start to brown,
they'll go quickly. Using a
slotted spoon, remove to
kitchen paper to drain and
crisp. Season with a scant
pinch of sea salt. Once cool,
they will keep in a jar for up
to 5 days. Keep the shalloty
oil, it's great for dressings
and cooking.

Velvety Onions

2 medium onions, peeled

25ml extra virgin olive oil

25g butter

1 tbsp finely chopped rosemary

¼ tsp sea salt

Halve the onions lengthways and slice them from tip to root. In a large frying pan, heat the oil and butter over a medium heat, add the onions and stir to combine. After 5 minutes the onions will have started to soften nicely; add the rosemary and salt and turn the heat down to low. Stir occasionally to prevent sticking, and if they catch add a tablespoon or two of water to loosen and incorporate the caramelised bits. The onions will be tender and velvety in 30 to 35 minutes.

Jammy Eggs

Bring a pan of salted water to the boil, add the eggs and boil gently for exactly 7 minutes, then cool them immediately in cold running water to halt the cooking process. When cool enough to handle, peel off the shells and cut them in half. Allow 10 minutes for hard boiled. If you make them in advance, keep them in the fridge for 2 to 3 days and reheat when needed by covering with boiling water for 10 minutes – this will be enough to warm through without cooking them further.

Quick Pickles

500g vegetable or fruit

for the pickling liquid:

250ml white wine vinegar

250ml water

2 tsp sea salt

2 tsp maple syrup

sprigs of dill, rosemary or thyme

1 tbsp of peppercorns and

1 tbsp each of mustard, coriander and fennel seeds

First sterilise your jars: preheat the oven to 140°C/120°C fan. Wash the jars and lids well then dry upside down in the oven for 15 minutes. Or put them through the hot cycle of a dishwasher. Chop your veggies into similar sized pieces and pack them tightly into the jar(s). Bring the pickling liquid to a boil and pour over the veggies until the jar is completely full. Tap the jar on the counter to shake loose any bubbles and screw the lid on tightly. Allow to cool before you refrigerate. The softer the vegetable, the faster they will pickle. I blanche green beans to fix the colour, and carrots and cauliflower to tenderise them. The soonest you could enjoy them is 2 hours, but they will last for at least 2 weeks in the fridge.

Some fave combos:

Strawberries and basil

Green beans, shallots, Szechuan pepper

Carrots and red onions

Cherries, vodka (instead of pickling liquid) and dill

Preserved Lemons or Limes

125g fine sea salt

50g caster sugar

8–10 thin-skinned lemons or limes washed in hot water

Have a large clean jar ready (see Quick Pickles, left, for how to sterilise). Mix the salt and sugar in a large bowl. Cut the lemons or limes into quarters without cutting all the way through so they are still joined at the bottom. Then, in the bowl, pack the salt mix into the cuts in each fruit and place in the jar. Once the jar is full, use a wooden spoon to press down and compact the fruit until they are completely submerged in their juices. Add more lemon or lime juice, if necessary, to ensure they are completely covered. Compact every day until everything is softened and submerged in the juices, then refrigerate for a month before using and store in the fridge for up to a year.

Choosing Leaves

Different leaves bring different textures and flavours to the salad party. Bags of mixed leaves are nice, and helpfully easy, but when you look further afield to fragrant herbs, juicy crunchy pea shoots or the peppery bite of rocket, the difference is transformative. Here are some of my favourites, categorised by flavour, so you can mix things up a bit.

Juicy	Peppery	Bitter
cos/romaine/ baby gem	rocket	radicchio
butterhead/round	red mustard	chicory
iceberg	mizuna	endive
sorrel	watercress	frisée
oak leaf	nasturtium	escarole
pea shoots	radish tops	baby dandelion

Index

Acknowledgements

Thank you to Sean Toner for his invaluable salad prepping work and assistance at the photo shoot and to Bethany Ferguson for her food prepping and styling skills behind the scenes at photography. Special thanks to Lynne Roberts of Italian ceramics and homewares shop Salento (www.salentoshop.co.uk) and to

Edinburgh-based ceramicist Sandra Brown (www.sandrabrownceramics.com) for the loan of the many beautiful handmade plates that feature throughout this book. Thank you to Garth Gulland of Roots, Fruits and Flowers in Glasgow for his help sourcing fruit and vegetables for photography.